Biography Of Sister Sarah Navaroji

Rev.Dr.R.SAMUEL

ISBN 978-93-5610-966-7
© Rev.Dr.R.SAMUEL 2022
Published in India 2022 by Pencil

A brand of
One Point Six Technologies Pvt. Ltd.
123, Building J2, Shram Seva Premises,
Wadala Truck Terminal, Wadala (E)
Mumbai 400037, Maharashtra, INDIA
E connect@thepencilapp.com
W www.thepencilapp.com

Author biography

Rev.Dr.R.Samuel,MIE(I),M.Th,Ph.D1

Rev.Dr.R. Samuel was born in the year 1952, in a well known town, Kancheepuram of Tamil Nadu,India to a C.S.I. Christian parents who have accepted the Lord Jesus Christ from a staunch Hindu background.It is a great testimony to tell how his father Late Mr.Ramachandran and his mother Late Mrs. Kirubavathi have come to the marvelous light of Christ from a life of darkness.

R.Samuel, a Post Graduate in Electrical Engineering has also obtained his Ph.D. (Doctorate Degree in Bible Studies) and Master Degree in Theology. Since being born and brought up in a disciplined and good Christian family, he was taught with the Bible systematically both at home and in the Church Sunday School.

Eventually, at God's appointed time he obeyed the Word of God (St.Matthew 28: 19, Colossians 2:12, Titus 3: 5, I Peter 5: 3,4) and took immersion water Baptism to enter into a New Life with the Lord Jesus Christ

After serving in the INDIAN NAVY in the Electrical Department for a prescribed period he worked in the MERCHANT NAVY as Electrical Officer, also worked in India and abroad in various industries as Electrical Engineer and Project Manager.

Wherever he was posted in his secular job, in all those places he made sure to join the nearby Full Gospel Churches and get involved in the Gospel ministry works. He has been fully engaged in learning the Bible correctly and teaching the same to others till today.

In the year 1982 he got married to the daughter of Sister Sarah Navaroji's elder Sister Lalitha Evangeline. Since then he has been a member of Zion Gospel Prayer Fellowship Church, Chennai, founded and led by Sister Sarah Navaroji and was involved in the Church activities.

It is this close relationship with Sister Sarah Navaroji that enabled him to get first hand information all about Sister Sarah Navaroji's Life and Ministry.

The author had submitted a thesis on the four fold ministries of Sister Sarah Navaroji for his Ph.D. degree to the University of Jerusalem .

Presently the Author Rev.Dr..R.Samuel is the Pastor-in-Charge of ZION GOSPEL PRAYER FELLOWSHIP CHURCH Fouunded by Sister Sarah Navaroji at 46-Kuttiappan 2nd Street, Kilpauk, Chennai- 600 010, India. The Extracts of this Book is also available in Tamil version for which the Author can be contacted in his mobile +91 9884713075 and email: rsam13in@yahoo.com

To God be the Glory ! Amen !

CONTENTS

INTRODUCTION

We have in the record many biographies of Christian Missionaries in India who were from foreign countries. Though many Missionaries from our own country have toiled in the Mission field not many biographies are on record about our Indian Missionaries. More so, very less about Women Christian Missionaries. This Book brings to limelight the works of a WOMAN CHRISTIAN MISSIOARY from Tamil Nadu whom God powerfully used in the 20th and 21st Century.

1.The Holy Bible says that the Gospel of Jesus Christ should be proclaimed and spread all over the world in all dimensions by men and women who are the disciples of Jesus according to Mathew 28: 18,19 & 20.,I Corinthians 9:16., II Timothy 4:2. Sister Sarah Navaroji, as a true disciple of Jesus has fully dedicated her life towards this cause as a Poetess, Preacher, Prophetess and Church Planter. The exemplary work done by her in this four fold ministry of the Lord would indeed provoke any true disciple of Jesus to launch into a dynamic ministry by reading this book.

2. In the history of mankind men have been dominating in almost every field and kept women aside except a very few examples down the centuries in India and other Countries.

However, in the recent times there has been an awakening among men and women folk alike that women should be given equal rights with men in public life. After the 18th Century the world Nations have truly witnessed that women had been raising to the occasion in each and every field to compete or rather support men towards the uplifting of human race in Political, Qualitative,Religious, Social and Technological fields.

As far as the Christian mission field is concerned, women are not strangers. Both in the Old Testamant and New Testamant times women have played vital role. Deborah, Ruth and Esther in the Old Testament and Mary, Lydia and Pricilla in the New Testament are some of the finest examples. In the Contemporary world also there have been many women who have played significant role in India and other countries such as Panditha Ramabai, Mary Cury and Mother Thereza to quote a few. There are many other women whose role in Gods mission are not recorded .

3. Hence it is necessary and a need of the hour to make a book of this sort on the ministries of Sister Sarah Navaroji as a women missionary of this, 20th and 21st century in the Lord's work who inspired many Christians and non-Christians and brought them into the fold of Jesus Christ. She has pioneered many leading men and women Servants of God who have done great works in the mission field of Jesus Christ. Furthermore, this documentary collection will definitely be a great treasure for the contemporary Christian world and to our next generation as well.

4. At first, the chapters detail Sister's early life and her induction into the Lords ministry. Then, the Subsequent

chapters explain about the manifold ministries of Sister Sarah Navaroji one by one of which the Song ministry is explained with portions of the actual songs elaborately.

All Glory, Honour and Praise be to God! Amen !

CHAPTER 1 -Early Life

Early Life of Sister Sarah Navaroji

1.1 Family Back Ground

Born to Christian Parents on 12th May 1938, namely, Solomon Asirvatham the Father and Soundaram Asirvatham the Mother ,Sister Sarah Navaroji is youngest in the family of four daughters. It was in the Egmore Children Hospital in Chennai which was then called Madras she was born. When the father came to Hospital to see his new born child, he was informed that he got a fair and beautiful girl child. This message that the fourth child also is a girl has annoyed him so much that he simply went back home without even looking at the baby. However, he brought up all his four daughters in good discipline, God fearing manner and provided all the necessary care and protection to them.

After the mother and child returned home from hospital, it so happened on the 10th day , mother Soundaram Asirvatham laid the baby on a cot in an open space out side the bedroom and went in to have her lunch. On her return she didn't find the child on the cot. She was so frightened that she cried and searched all over the surrounding places only to find the baby wrapped in a cloth lying underneath the cot and sleeping peacefully. Almighty's protection was on Sister Sarah Navaroji even from the days of her birth. It so became that the father loved this youngest daughter more than other children.

Solomon Asirvatham once heard the discourse given by Sadhu Sunder Singh in a Gospel meeting that has made a lasting impact on him towards serving the Lord. Sister Sarah Navaroji's Grand Father Solomon, father of Solomon Asirvatham had four brothers and one sister. They were from a Land Lord family of Nadukkottai, Thirumangalm in Madurai District. Their father Subbaiah Thevar was well known by his nick name in Tamil called 'Puliyodu Kattippuranda Subbaiah Thevar', meaning 'Subbaiah Thevar who had encounter with a Tiger'.

It so happened one day when Subbaiah Thevar was inspecting his vast Land possession, a tiger came roaring to attack him. While those who were with him have fled the scene ,he bravely fought with the tiger.During the course of that fight, he and the tiger literally rolled one over the other on the ground and hence he was conferred with this title after his name. Even though Subbaiah Thever received some bruises and tears in his skin, he inflicted heavy injury to the tiger and it died eventually. He preserved the tooth of the tiger for a long time.

1.2 Conversion of the Grand Parents to Christianity

Subbaiah Thevar, his five sons and one daughter were all from a staunch Hindu family. They were so much devoted to the Hindu religion that they were also responsible for bringing the much revered god Alagar's idol to the Alagar temple in Madurai and perform special pujas (worships). However, according to the verse in the Holy Bible I Peter 2:9

'You are a chosen generation,............that you may proclaim the praises of Him who called you out of darkness into His marvelous light;'

God has chosen the children of Subbaiah Thevar, and called them out of the darkness of idol worship to the great light of the world Lord Jesus Christ to proclaim His praise through their true

Christian lives and devotional songs. It is by the ministry of a missionary namely Bishop Sanda Green all the five brothers and one sister came to know the love of Jesus. They all had converted to Christianity and joined Lutheran Mission Church. The five brothers are Solomon (Sister Sarah Navaroji's grand Father), his other brothers are namely Muthuswamy, Arulanandam, Samuel, Bakkyam and the Sister Thangathai. They all testified the love of Jesus to their relatives and friends and did bring many souls to the Lord. One of the brothers Muthuswamy was a Reverend (Priest)in Lutheran Mission.

1.3 The Poetic Gift of Grand Fathers

Sister Sarah Navaroji's grand Father Solomon and other brothers all had the poetic gift. They are all good devotional song writers. Not only that but also their gift was so tremendous that they had the skill of writing songs instantly.

Solomon had a daughter elder to Solomon Asirvatham (Father of Sister Navaroji) namely Ponnuthai. She was a teacher and an Evangelist. She had a son born to her after many years whom she loved more than any else thing in her life. At the age of three ,this beloved son died and due to this bereavement her husband became mentally ill. Owing to this miserable circumstance she was very much dejected in life and went into solitary confinement refusing to be comforted by any one. At this instant, Rev.Muthuswamy , brother of Solomon (Ponnuthai's Uncle) went to meet and give counseling to her. But she refused to open the door of her room. Instantly, a great historic song proceeded from the depth of his heart and he started . It is this well known song which he composed and sung at that instant that has been comforting down the years so many Christian believers in their sorrow till to-day.

> Oru Pothum maravaadha
> Unmai Pitha irukka
> Unakkenna kuraivundu? Maganeh! Magaleh!
> Siruvan thottunnaiyoru
> Chella pillaipole kaatha
> Urimai thanthai yendrendrum
> Uyirodiruppaar nambu.
> (meaning)
> When you have a true Father
> Who never forgets you
> What do you lack? My son!My daughter!
> Since your childhood
> Like a beloved child he protected you!
> The same rightful Father is alive
> For ever more ! believe !

This song made a miraculous change in the mind set of Ponnuthai that she came out to meet her uncle Muthuswamy and was comforted by him.

His brother Solomon (Sister Navaroji's grand Father) also had the talent of instant composing of songs apt to the situation. Solomon's son Solomon Asirvatham and his daughter-in-law Soundaram Asirvatham were coming to his house as a newly wedded couple. Solomon, at the instant of receiving his son and daughter-in-law, then and there, composed a song and received them. The song goes like this,

> Muppathorandaiyum
>> Murumurppillamal
>> Karputhanai kaathukonda
>> En kadai maganeh!

> (meaning)
>> For thirty one years
>> Without grumbling
>> Maintained your integrity,O!
>> My last son!

Thus he welcomed his last son Solomon Asivatham upon his wedded arrival,

commending his son's patient endurance for thirty one years of life leading a pure

bachelor's life.

These are one or two specimens but there are many more such songs composed by these divine gifted brothers..

1.4 Father's Passion for Carnatic Music

Young Solomon Asirvatham2

Solomon Asirvatham Father of Sister Navaroji was a violinist, student of renowned

violinist Chaudhiya who inturn was the disciple of the famous violinist Dwaram

Venkataswamy Naidu. Solomon Asirvatham was also working as a teacher in

Lutheren High Schools at Pudukottai and Madras where he use to teach carnatic music

as well. He also taught music to the Under trainee Gurukkals (Pastors) of Lutheren Church. He was so fond of music that he named his three of the four daughters after the carnatic ragas namely Lalitha, Vasantha and Navaroji. He Composed carnatic ragas for the Christian Songs. He taught his daughters carnatic music and did not like them to sing light music or western music songs. It is a great testimony that the children also learnt the music with passion that they gained expertise. Sister Sarah Navaroji's elder sister Lalitha has learnt veena and obtained a Diploma in music.

Solomon Asirvatham use to conduct Gospel Music concerts in the Luthren church very often. He use to practice at home in preparation for this concerts with the musical instruments such as violin, Mirthangam etc. Since his daughters have kept listening to his practicing songs from their early ages, they acquired the talent of good singing. Sister Sarah Navaroji even at the age of three was known to be singing a certain Lyric (Keerthanai) song of 'Aaberi raga' , a carnatic tune, so perfectly without any mistake that they use to make her sing in front of many audience.

Once when Solomon Asirvatham took his children to their grand mothers house, there he was playing his violin on 'thodi raga' a famous carnatic tune till late in the night. Suddenly,noticing a snake right in front of him being charmed by the music was dancing, the person with him shouted saying Snake! Snake!. Solomon Asirvatham instead of stopping his violin play at once, had gradually slowed down and halted.

The snake struck the ground three times with its head and left the place without harming any one. It was by the grace of God the presence of mind of Solomon Asirvatham and his expertise on the instrument had protected the people around him from a great danger that day.

Apart from learning the carnatic music systematically from her father, Sister Sarah Navaroji had a natural melodious voice from the beginning. As the Lord God said in
The Holy Bible,
'This people have I formed for myself; they shall show forth my praise.'
Isaiah 43:21

There is no doubt that it is the Lord himself has chosen this generation even from their grand parents to show forth the praise and glory of God to the world through their songs and music. The Almighty has indeed enabled them by providing necessary skill and gifts for this noble purpose.

1.5 Raised up Under Mother's Care

Soundaram Asirvatham3

In the year 1948 at the tender age of 10, Sister Navaroji has lost her father. At the death bed, Solomon Asirvatham listening to Dwaram Venkatasamy Naidu's violin music in the radio, he made movements by his fingers as if he is playing violin and said with a smiling face 'in a short while I will be in Zion (heaven) and play my violin there. But Sister Sarah Navaroji was so much disappointed and disgusted to realize that she will never again listen to the melodious violin notes of her father. Little did she foresaw that one day God will raise her up to be a world renown composer and singer of many divine melodious songs for the glory of Lord Jesus Christ. After the earthly demise of the father, the whole burden of family care came on the shoulders of the mother. They then started attending brethren mission Church in Madras. Soundaram Asirvatham who was taking care of her four daughters, was working as a teacher in C.S.I Preparatory School,Kilpauk, Madras.

Soundaram Asirvatham was so thirst for doing Lords ministry that she eventually started Child Evangelism along with a western lady namely Hilda Ekman. They use to collect children from streets and slums and teach them songs of the Lord and Bible stories. They use to distribute to the poor children eatables and clothes , keeping up with the well known principle of Soap, Soup and Salvation and showing the love of Jesus to the poor and down trodden. Soundaram Asirvatham resigned her job as a teacher and began her full time child evangelism ministry after her youngest daughter Sister Sarah Navaroji completed her high school studies(S.S.L.C).

In the Brethren Mission Church also the four daughters started singing songs as they use to do in the Lutheren Church.

Mother with four daughters4

In the year 1950, some missionaries came from America and were astonished to hear the melodious songs sung by this four young girls and requested them that they would like to record their singing. They eventually carried the recorded songs to America and distributed them there. The Western missionaries who were doing village ministries in Tamil Nadu also used these recorded songs in their village ministries and street preaching .

As all the songs were in Carnatic music tune, people from other religion also use to like and enjoy listening to this songs.

CHAPTER 2 - Her Salvation and Ministry

**Personal Salvation and Induction into the
Lord's Ministry of Sister Sarah Navaroji**

2.1 Vision

Sister had a vision in her dream one night in which she saw a junction of four cross roads and a Policeman showing the direction. He told her that if she took the broad way, she will go to hell and that the other narrow road will take her to heaven. Hence, she opted the narrow road. She started walking through the narrow road alone. The people who were going through the broad road mocked and pelted stones at her. As she was walking lonely on the narrow road she saw number of crosses erected all along the way. She took refuge behind these crosses to protect herself from the stones being hurled by the broad road walkers every time they attacked her. At that instant, she heard a voice saying "My daughter climb up and come.". Then, she saw a hand lifting her gently up the steps to a very highest level where she saw the one who was looking glorious and shining in all brilliance. With fear and trembling she asked who he was and the glorious one replied saying"I am JESUS".She cried bitterly and clung to His feet. In the morning ,on getting up she saw her pillow fully wet with tears and told her mother about the dream. After some days, in a convention meeting held by the bretheren mission church she fully surrendered herself to accept Christ as her personal Saviour at the age of fourteen. Then on, she started spending many hours in prayer to know the will of God for her future life.

2.2 Heavenly Vision

After Sister Sarah Navaroji completed her School final (S.S.L.C) and was learning type writing, one day she went to attend a youth meeting for sisters in the nearby C.P.M church. At the time of prayer she saw a vision. Jesus Christ appeared as crucified on the cross and asked her a question 'My daughter ! I bore the heavy rugged cross for you. What have you done for me?. Hearing this voice,sister Navaroji wept and surrendered herself fully to the Lord and came back home. The next day early morning,she went to the open terrace in her house with the Bible and started praying. Then at that instance the heavens have opened and an angel took her to a very high place above the skies. At the end she saw a huge mansion and to climb up there red carpet of had been spread. The floor of the mansion was made of pure gold and the walls were impregnated with precious stones.

Sister Sarah narrates her experience there in that heavenly place:-

" I was so frightened and hesitant to go inside the mansion and step on that floor because it was made of expensive pure gold which I valued so much that I am wearing the same gold jewellry as my ornaments. Suddenly on hearing a voice calling me 'you, come in' I went inside. I heard a loud voice and asked the angel who accompanied me there what it was. The angel answered and said to me 'this is the voice of many God's people praying from the earth. If you go back to the earth and pray your voice also will be heard here'. So saying he pushed me down to earth and I flew back to the open terrace of my house. There I saw my body leaning over the Bible and lying. As soon as I touched my body I rose up and I felt numbness all over my frame. When I went down to my house my mother asked me 'did you not go to the type writing class?'.

I answered her saying ' I went to heaven and came back'. My mother replied 'I knew that you will become mad when you have gone to that C.P.M church meeting'. In those days my mother did not know about such experiences as she was still attending brethren mission church.

The angel who accompanied Sister Navaroji in the mansion had told her that she cannot come to that mansion except she get immersed and pass through water.

2.3 Immerse Baptism and Anointing of the Holy Spirit

Sister Navaroji had a maternal uncle namely Thomas who was a minister in the CPM church. Sister was very much influenced by him and he lead her to take the immerse Baptism in Water at the age of sixteen. He also taught her about the Holy Spirit anointing. Sister had many doubts about this subject. So,she took fasting and prayed nearly for a month. One day she alone went to the near by CPM church and prayed with tears. Suddenly she heard a voice telling her " tomorrow at 3 'O, Clock I will anoint you." The next day she went to the Church with her sister and both prayed for the anointing of the Holy Spirit. First, her sister received the anointing of the Holy Spirit. So,Sister Navaroji stood up there and asked the Lord to anoint her also with the Holy Spirit. Immediately, she saw angels surrounding her and the Holy Spirit was poured upon her powerfully. God spoke to her saying,

"I have no beauty on the cross, but you are making yourself beautiful.

 I have taken the cruel cross for you. What have you done for me ?"

On hearing that she said,

 " Lord , I surrender myself to you".

She also heard the angels singing a wonderful song and it was from Psalm

Chapter 91.As she was hearing this melodious singing the famous song from Psalm 91

in Tamil sprang forth from the depth of her heart with the heavenly tune.

She composed the following song then and there.

"Unnadha maanavarin – uyarmaraivillirukkiravan

  Sarvavallavarin nizhallil thanguvaan

  Idhu paramasillakkiyame."

(meaning)

 " He who dwells in the shelter of the most High

  Shall rest in the shadow of the Almighty

  This is a great privilege."   Song No.120

So, it is crystal clear that along with the anointing of the Holy Spirit, God gave her the gift of composing divine inspired songs.

This is an early song that was composed, tuned and sung by Sister Sarah Navaroji which has become a hit song all over the world and being delightfully sung even to-day by all Christians without any denominational barrier.

After this incident both sisters re-dedicated themselves to the Lord in a total submission and also made a covenant with Jesus to wear white dress only.

Sister Navaroji was wearing jewels at that time. She had three reasons why she was wearing Jewels. However, God convinced her that this three reasons are not valid and

gave answers from appropriate Bible verses for all the three reasons. Then, Sister

removed her jewels never to wear them again.

Her reason: To enhance my beauty.

God's Answer: While being nailed to the cross I had no beauty. Why do You

adorn   yourself ?. I Peter 3 : 3.

Her reason : It is the symbol of social status.

God's Answer: That which is highly esteemed among men is an abomination in the sight of God. Luke : 16 : 15

Her reason : It is the source of money in need.

God's Answer : Do not worry about tomorrow. Mathew 6 : 34

2.4 Employment in Madras Electricity Service

During these days, Sister Navaroji was unemployed and was Praying for a job. She wrote MPSC (Madras Public Service Commission) exam and the result came as failed, though Sister was confident that she will pass. As she continued in prayer another result came nullifying the previous one saying that she passed and an appointment letter will follow. But no appointment order came for several days. Dejected, sister decided to fast and pray. She fasted and prayed for a month. It was the

31st day of fasting and no any sign of appointment order or postman seen even as the day was going to end and it was 5.00 p.m. Sister was so much upset and bitterly cried and prayed to the Lord. She didn't know whether to end the fast or continue. But God who hears the prayers of his children in spite of the many obstacles put forth by the adversary, has done a miracle that night. A man(not Post man) with the appointment order of Sister Navaroji from Madras Electricity Service came to her

house searching for her. On finding who is Ms.Sarah Navaroji,he said that the MES Office staff forgot to post this appointment letter that says she must join duty the next day. Because the Officer-in- Charge of MES Office was so angry on his staff for their negligence and ordered them to deliver the appointment letter somehow to the concerned person that night itself, the man came rushing to give the letter to Sister and apologized for the inconvenience caused. Furthermore, he requested Sister that without fail she should join duty the next morning. It was an appointment in the Madras Electricity Service at the CEIG office. Sister Navaroji her elder sisters and mother were so delighted to realize how God loved her so much and did this great miracle overnight according to the God's word in the Holy Bible,

' Do not be anxious (worried) about anything, but in everything,   by   prayer   and   petition,   with thanksgiving,present your requests to God.'

Philippians 4:6

The man who delivered the letter to Sister told everyone in the office next morning that one Bible woman is going to join duty that day because he saw her with Bible while delivering the letter to her.

In order to enquire about the long delay in receiving the appointment letter from MES, Sister Sarah Navaroji along with her mother went to the TNPSC office. The explanation given by the TNPSC office was furthermore surprising to both of them.

After allotting jobs to all the TNPSC Exam passed candidates ,there were 10 more vacancies still remaining to be filled up. So, they chose 10 top candidates from the failed list in which Sister Navaroji was the 10th. It was as if God directly intervened to get Sister Sarah an appointment even though her name did not appear in the first list. This miraculous testimony had been very much inspiring to many believers. Sister Sarah Navaroji joined (CEIG) the Head Office of Madras Electricity Service in Madras. Always she would have a Bible on her desk. During lunch time she will read the Bible and while returning home from the office everyday she used to spend time in Gospel tracts distribution at the bus terminus with much burden.

Also, she use to directly and indirectly let know about her Lord Jesus to all the staff in the office, from the senior ranking officers to the junior most employee . It use to be a regular practice that they in turn ask her to pray to Jesus for there problems and needs.

2.5 Dedication to the Lord's service

Sister Navaroji was attending CPM Church in these days after her Baptism in Water and Spirit there. In a Church service during prayer, the Chief Pastor of the CPM Church Pastor.Alwin has chosen Sister Navaroji and her other elder Sister Vasantha for the ministry.One day, when Sister was praying at morning 4 O'Clock, she heard a voice saying " Take up the cross and follow me". Also she had a vision in which she saw her own resignation letter. Underneath the letter, instead of her signature she found the word written Mathew 10th Chapter, which says about the Lord sending out his twelve disciples into the ministry. Understanding that the Lord is calling her for ministry, she resigned her job from MES.Her elder sister Vasantha also resigned her job after some days to enter into the Lord's ministry.Both sisters joined the CPM church to serve as sisters in the ministry. Sister Navaroji was posted in Ceylon and her elder Sister Vasantha was posted in Madras. Sister Navaroji landed in Ceylon on 11th June 1960 to start her ministry with CPM Church. During her ministerial service in Ceylon with the CPM Church she spent many hours in fervent prayer & meditation. God continued to bless her with the special gift of composing divine inspired songs. Recognizing the gift of composing songs, the church Pastors there have entrusted her with the service of composingTamil songs. Sister Sarah Navaroji's composed songs were accepted by many church authorities since they knew that the songs were given from heaven.During these days, some disturbing situations started in the CPM Church, Ceylon. Hearing about the commotion there, Sister Navaroji's mother and her eldest sister Chandra Leela who was an officer in the Passport Office along with her husband

Pushparaj went to Ceylon to bring Sister Navaroji back to Madras. It was very difficult to get her released from Ceylon because all Indians passport were kept under the Ceylonese Government custody. Since Sister's Eldest Sister Chandra Leela was a Passport Officer in Madras she could arrange for the release of her passport. It was indeed another miracle. In fact, Sister Navaroji was not willing to leave her ministry in Ceylon CPM Church in spite of the troubled atmosphere there. But they forcibly brought her back to Madras against her wishes in the year 1962 never to go back to Ceylon.

It is surprising to note that the period of Sister Sarah Navaroji served in C.P.M Church, Ceylon is exactly 2 years i.e (11th June 1960 to 12th June 1962).

CHAPTER 3 - Church Ministry

CHAPTER 3
Church Ministry
3.1 Introduction

" And we know that in all things God works for the good of those who love Him who
have been called according to His purpose." Romans 8: 28. Since Sister Sarah Navaroji was a chosen vessel called by God for His purpose, the changes took place in her life worked out for the good according to the above Bible verse. Even though she was so sad to leave Ceylon and that the ministerial service she was doing in CPM Church was to be abruptly abandoned, God had greater plans for her towards the ministerial works she will be carrying out in the later days about which little did she realize at that time.

According to the Bible verse,
'Faithful is he that called you…..' I Thessalonians 5: 24
God who called her never had let any circumstances or disturbances to disrupt the purpose of His high calling in her life.

" He who has begun a good work in you will carry it on to completion
until the day of Christ Jesus." Philippians 1: 6.

Rightly as this Bible verse says, God who started a good work from the early life of Sister has been mindful of carrying on to accomplish each and every ministry to be done by her till the day of Christ Jesus. God had a great plan to plant many churches through her ministry in and around Tamil Nadu and in some foreign countries.

However, Sister Navaroji did not have any Master plan about her future ministry after returning to Madras. But things started unfolding one by one and God was sending appropriate persons time to time to prompt her and help her to initiate and proceed with the God intended ministries. It was the total dedication, spiritual sensitivity, physical sacrifices and obedience to God's voice by Sister that saw her doing and completing the task set before her by the Lord. It should also be added here that Sister kept up the same consecration she made at the start of her ministry till to-day and remained as a Spinster to serve the Lord with all her heart and with all her soul and with all her mind.

In those early years after the independence of India, there were very few churches in India and that too Full Gospel teaching Churches were sparse. Even after so many years the so called Christian churches in forefront have not experienced the power and outpouring of the Holy Spirit. They still were practicing various ways of heathen and satisfied with their social works. Those Churches that taught about the salvation, separated holy life,Lord's second coming.,doing God's will in the day to day life, eternal life were very few. More over, these two kinds of churches never mingled with each other.

However, according to the prophecy of prophet Haggai ,

'The glory of this latter house shall be greater than the former..' Haggai 2:9

The Spirit of God descended with zeal to fulfill this promise in the Churches.

It would not be an exaggeration to say that God with his mighty hand and an outstretched arm lifted up Sister Sarah Navaroji ,a young women, in his right hand and used her in Tamil Nadu and other states of India to plant the churches on the foundation of the early Apostle's doctrines and to remove the darkness covering them. With the mighty anointing of the Holy Spirit she stormed into the Christian mission field and preached unadulterated Gospel stressing the need for repentance, immerse Baptism in the water and the anointing of the Holy Spirit.

To those who preached and taught that Social Service and a good moral life is only required, Sister Navaroji pointed out the Bible verse,

'Our righteousness are as fithy rages…..' Isaiah 64:6

and highlighted the Lord's sermon on the mount (Mathew 5: 16,19) where the Lord says it is necessary to do good works as well as to keep all God's commandments and thus heralded to prepare the Church as a suitable bride for Christ.

Many who opposed her straight forward preaching of the correct doctrine at the beginning, have later fell in line with her teaching of the unadulterated word of God.

Eventhough , many hypocritical teachings, fierce and slanderous allegations, murderous conspiracies have opposed her, Sister Sarah Navaroji wore her apostolic calling as a crown from God and the malicious words hurled at her as a badge of honour remembering the Masters saying in

Mathew   5:11,

'Blessed are you when people insult you, persecute you and falsely say all kinds of evil against you because of me.'

If this could be said that ,she the bold Apostle, not being intimidated by any of these threats but marched forward to plant many Churches on the sure foundation of Christ and his firm teachings, we can well conclude that women have had their right share in the mission field of Christ.

It is amazing to witness in the history of the Church that time and again the Holy Spirit has been raising true Servants of God like Martine Luther to reform the Church of Jesus Christ. Sister Sarah Navaroji is one in that list for the 20th century. Not only that but also by her relentless ministry she had prepared many a true servants of God who faithfully work for the continuous reformation and revival of Churches the bride of Christ.

3.2 Church Founding

On 12th June 1962, Sister Sarah Navaroji has landed in Madras along with her mother, eldest Sister Chandra Leela Pushparaj and Brother-in-law Pushparaj. Sister Navaroji stayed in the house of her elder Sister Lalitha Evangeline's family at Kilpauk area in a street namely Kuttiappan Gramani Street along with her mother. She had no Master Plan about the type of ministries that she will be doing from here. She started a small prayer meeting in their house.

A surprising incident took place at that time. The chief Pastor of CPM Church Pastor.Alwin had come down to Madras from Ceylon to visit the CPM Churches in Madras. By God's guidance he came to the house where Sister Navaroji stayed and prayed for her. After praying, he delivered a prophetic word of the Lord and said to Sister

" You will start a Church and a faith home here." Again he said twice

" This will happen." It did happen in the later days.

The small prayer meeting she was conducting has become a small Prayer Fellowship.

People started coming regularly for this Prayer Fellowship meetings. The Lord began to answer the fervent prayers of his children gathering in this fellowship, comforting and consoling them and day by day they were growing in their faith.

3.3 Zion Gospel Prayer Fellowship Church

Eventually, this Prayer Fellowship started functioning as a church under the name "ZION GOSPEL PRAYER FELLOWSHIP CHURCH."

According to the Biblical pomise,

'Enlarge the place of thy tent, and let them stretch forth the curtains of thine habitations' Isaiah 54: 2

The Lord worked mightily and expanded the place of the Church Fellowship.

The Lord also added more and more souls day by day who were being saved through the anointed messages and earnest prayers of Sister Sarah Navaroji , the Founder and Leader of this Church. The Fellowship which started with just two families started growing in numbers day by day. The Lord also expanded the area of church premises.Mother Soundaram Asirvatham also was a great help and a guide in the ministry.

3.4 Church Growth

Sister Sarah Navaroji was very alert to listen to the voice of the Lord in her ministry. As she sensed the guidance of the Lord towards the growth of the Church,She took another step forward from the in-house prayer meeting to a public

Gospel meeting in a nearby open ground in the Kilpauk area called as 'Alleluah Ground' in those days opposite to the Kilpauk ESI Hospital. In the years 1967 and 1968 during the months of May and June for 10 days continuously Sister Sarah Navaroji preached the Gospel with anointed songs and prophetical words. People from near by Kilpauk, Ayanavaram, Purasaiwalkam areas and also those who heard from many other areas have come and attended these Gospel meetings. Even those who happen to pass by that place have been drawn towards word of God and were saved being touched by the Power of God. Likewise all those who were saved in these meetings have joined Zion Gospel Prayer Fellowship Church, took immerse water Baptism and were anointed by the Holy Spirit.

'I will give you every place where you set your foot'Joshua 1:3

According to this promise of God in the Holy Bible, Sister Navaroji as a next step decided to hold public Gospel campaign at place near Central Railway station which is the center of Madras city and a near to her church. From the year 1969 to 1975 in the open land known as S.I.A.A grounds near Moore Market located near the Madras Central Railway Station during the month of May or June Sister Sarah Navaroji conducted Gospel meetings for 7 to10 days continuously. People who participated in these meetings and witnessed many miracles and received blessings have become members of Zion Gospel Prayer Fellowship Church as individuals and families.

Those who joined the fellowship are the people who were delivered from the evil spirit Possession, idol worship, false belief and also from the verge of committing suicide due to various problems in life. There were well educated, uneducated, highly placed officials, ordinary people, men and women of different kinds.

Such people took part in the church worship service regularly and many among them have dedicated their lives for full time ministry and are now serving the Lord all over the world.

During the years 1962 to 1968 a servant of God ,Pastor. Maharaja Prasangiar had been helping Sister Navaroji in the Church functioning by performing the Baptism and Holy Communion services. He had arranged many Gospel campaigns for Sister Sarah Navaroji in Tirunelveli District.

3.5 The Lord Confirms Church Ministry

Every year before conducting the Public Gospel Meetings in S.I.A.A Grounds Sister Sarah Navaroji use to fast for 40 days and pray. In those days there were some who opposed the Church ministry of Sister for various reasons. So, to know the definite will of the Lord about her Church ministry Sister Navaroji fasted and prayed for 80 days. During the period of fasting she will only take fruit juice and water occasionally. She will lock her room inside and remain in prayer. On the 80th day of her fasting, while she was feeling extremely weak , she heard some one knocking at the door from outside and enquired 'who is there?'. Hearing two persons talking outside the room she came near to the door crawling since she did not have enough strength to walk. She kept her ear near the door and trying to hear what the persons outside were talking,but she could not understand their language. So, she requested them to talk in English or in Tamil and also asked them in which language they are conversing. Then one of them said that they spoke in Hebrews and also translated what they spoke in Tamil. He also read a portion from the Bible which was,

'I am the Almighty God; walk before me and be thou perfect....

I will multiply thee exceedingly.' Genesis 17: 1,2

Sister Navaroji was infact reading the same portion from the Bible at that time. Then she asked 'who are you speaking to me?'The person replied 'I am Jesus'. On hearing this words Sister fell fainted on the ground. After a long time she got up and found no one outside the door and was so upset that she did not invite the Master inside the room.

The Bible portion that The Lord read for her has confirmed about the Church Ministry she was doing. So, She ended her fasting and without any ambiguity she continued to build up the Church.

3.6 Pond of Wastewater becomes Place of Worship and
      Miryclay Pit becomes Mighty Pulpit

The Church premises at 46-Kuttiappan 2nd Street, Kipauk, Chennai-10 had a waste water pond at the backyard without any use. The Church congregation that was gathering within the house needed a big hall .Hence, Sister Sarah decided to convert this water pond as a ground to construct the Church hall . All the Church members worked together, filled the water pond with rubbish materials and debris and converted it as a ground. Upon this ground they constructed a big hall with cement flooring and thatched roof . Also there was a miry clay pit upon which the mighty pulpit had been erected to preach the word of God . Necessary lighting and Public Address System were installed. The Church Services were conducted in this hall.

'Every valley shall be filled.........all flesh shall see
 the Salvation of God.' Luke 3: 5,6.

This word of God has literally got fulfilled in 'Zion Gospel Prayer fellowship Church' at this premises. Even as the empty pit got filled to become a mighty platform for delivering the powerful word of God , multitude of people have heard message of salvation and received fullness of life from their emptiness being flooded with the Love of Jesus.

Pastor.Maharaja Prasangiar who was helping in the Church services was unable to continue after few years.Then Pastor . Nathan use to help Sister in the Pastoral functions of the Church such as Holy Communion and Baptism services. Later when Pastor.Nathan discontinued , Pastor.Lazer whom Sister Sarah Navaroji met at Kanyakumari district during her Gospel Campaign in those areas was invited to come to Zion Gospel Prayer Fellowship Church for conducting Baptism and Holy Commuion Services. every month on first Sunday to minister Holy Communion and Water Baptism. Upon Pastor.Lazer invitation Sister Navaroji had been visiting Mathur every year to preach in the annual convention meeting from the year 1968 to 2003.Along with Sister a group of brothers and sisters would go to Mathur to attend and help in the meetings. It is this long association with Pastor Lazarus that helped the Zion Gospel Prayer Fellowship Church to have his blessed Pastoral Services till to-day.

3.7 Z.G.P.F.Church Developments and other Ministerial activities.

The waste water stagnant place that changed to house the Zion Gospel Prayer fellowship Church Hall with thatched roof ,bamboo poles and small surrounding walls had under gone many a transformation over the years. To-day this hall stands completely renovated with fully extended walls, permanent roofing, false ceiling, flooring, and gates now stands as a concrete building where Church worship services are being held.

Similarly, a great number of believers who came to Jesus with their lives of wasted days and stagnation , after hearing the anointed messages of God through Sister Sarah Navaroji have had their lives changed from the state of being forsaken to inherit a fullness of blessed life in the Lord as this Bible promise says,

'Thou shall no more be termed forsaken;
neither shall thy land any more be termed desolate'
but thou shalt be called Hephzibah,and thy land Beulah:
for the Lord delighteth in thee…' Isaiah 62:4

In this dedicated Church Hall not only Sunday services but also many Special revival meetings had been conducted and many anointed servants of God from all over the world have come and preached the word of God. Further more, Wedding Services, Funeral Services and a lot of special functional services have been conducted for the glory of God and the edification of God's people visiting from all over.

Sister Sarah Navaroji has been delivering God's messages on every Sunday services except those days when she was out stations for preaching in various crusades. Her song ministry also continued in this place. Composing new songs, recording, releasing cassettes, CDs have also been done from this house only . New souls are being added to the church day after day and year after year. Sister

Navaroji's songs that were recorded in CDs have been recorded in MP3 formats and as the technology getting advanced, from the year 2010 these songs are recorded in Video DVDs and are made available.

The ingredients of Sisters messages are Prophecy, Preaching to edify, Bible Study, admonishing, consoling, casting out fear etc. It would be amazing to come across many believers of her congregation, who are illiterate, knowing and quoting the Scripture verses fluently. Such capacity is imparted to them not by any regular Bible study classes but only by listening to the messages delivered by her on Sunday services and singing the songs composed by her.

This fact clearly indicates that Sister's messages on Sundays in the church and her

songs cover completely the history, theology, doctrines and the Gospel contained in

the Old and New Testaments of the Holy Bible.

It is to be mentioned here again that many of the people who attended the Sunday services here and heard the messages delivered by Sister had in later days became well known Preachers, Pastors and Evangelists who have wrought great works for the Lord, though mentioning their names here will not be appropriate.

Presently, the Church worship services are conducted here every Sunday in the morning 10.30 A.M to 2.00 P.M .During the week days brothers group and sisters group gather in the evening 7.00 P.M to 9.00 P.M for intercessory prayers every day. They pray for various important points such as prayer requests that pour in, revival of Churches all over the world, spreading of the Gospel and destruction of devils work all over the world.

Sunday School classes are conducted by Church members to teach the Word of God to children every Sunday. At the end of every year Sunday School retreat is held for the Children to exhibit their talents and also show what they have learnt in the year long Sunday classes by means of drama, memory verse reciting and singing etc. Children are given prizes for good performances.

Youth Fellowship is a separate wing of the Church to encourage, train and revive youths in the church. Elders in the Church lead and guide them to learn the Word of God. They are trained in Village ministries, tracts distribution, conducting Prayer meetings, Preaching word of God etc.Young men of the youth fellowship meet on every 2nd Saturday in the evening from 5.00 p.m to 8.00 p.m and young women of the youth fellowship meet on every 4th Sunday 2.30 p.m to 3.30 p.m. Time to time on public holidays a combined youth camp is held for both young men and women of the youth fellowship.

Brothers group go out for hospital ministries every week on a particular day and to village ministries, street preaching on public holidays. Special Prayer meetings are conducted in the believers houses for instances such as house dedication, birthday blessings, and any special thanks giving occasions. Special Church services are conducted on festival occasions such as Christmas, Good Friday and Easter. A general invitation is extended to Christians and non-Christians through News paper advertisement and personal invitation to attend these services. The purpose of these special meetings is to preach the Gospel to all the invited people on the pretext of festival celebration.

The New Year watch night service is an important occasion in the Church.A glorious worship service is conducted from 10.30 p.m of the old year to 4.30 a.m of the New year. All the member believers from all the branch churches will come to the main church and it will be a combined worship.

Pastor Lazarus also will come to this New year watch night service and conduct Holy Communion and Baptism services. The whole family of God will enter into the New Year with one accord and one mind lead by Sister Sarah Navaroji in Praise and Prayer. Inspired by the Holy Spirit she will Prophecy and tell the Church what God wants to say to his people on the event of inheriting a New Year.

A lot of new comers who are not regular members of this church also come to attend this glorious worship service, some being invited and some on their own accord. Special promise words from the Bible verse also given through prophecy to the believers at that instance. After the New Year service, all believers go out energy packed entering into a fresh and bright blessed year to live and work for the Lord.

The Zion Gospel Prayer Fellowship Church functioning in 46- Kuttiappan 2nd Street, Kilpauk, Chennai-10 has seen many Special meetings, Crusades and Revival meetings held in the same premises for the glory of the Lord. Many foreign missionaries have visited and took part in these special meetings and in Sunday worship services also.

3.7.1. WITNESSES

Here are some beloved Children of God Witnessing for How God transformed their lives through this Church Ministry as a few sample testimonies for the multitude of souls blessed.

a) AQUILA and PRISCILLA Couple

My name was Saraswathy. I was born in the year 1947, 29th November to Hindu Parents namely Ganapathy Raman and Kokilammal.

In the year 1965, my Father had a sudden chest pain and doctors declared that he will die within hours. He was the sole bread winner of our home and so I was shocked and worried very much.Immediately I went into our puja (prayer) room and prayed to all the known Hindu gods to save the life of my Father. At that moment I heard a voice from a distance floating in the air and coming to my ears, may be it was from a Christian meeting going on some where that I don't know, and some one proclaimed that Jesus says

' Come to me, all you who are weary and burdened, and I will give you rest.'

Later I came to know this is a Bible verse.(Mathew 11:28). On hearing this, I felt a great relief and a peace descended in my heart. I felt like a big burden has rolled away from my back. Immediately,I prayed to Lord Jesus to save the life of my Father. My father survived and later I shared this experience with one of my Christian friend. She gave me a Bible and asked me to read it daily. I was steadily learning about the Christian Truths and the Love of Lord Jesus Christ who is the only true God. My father did not like my faith in Christianity.

In the year 1966, I passed my S.S.L.C (High School Final)and in the year 1970, I got a State Govt. job in Cuddalur by the grace of Lord Jesus.After two years, my father got me married to an Hindu husband who was very devoted to Hindu gods. His name was Kani Irullappan and he also started opposing my devotion to Jesus and faith in Christianity. Within a year son was born to us.

After two years a girl baby was born to us. Our son was named Moses and daughter as Lydia. She was born without the knee cap on her left leg and the leg could be bent forward and back ward like a rubber tube. She could not walk till 1 ½ years of age. The child also had eczema skin disease and the hairs turned white. My husband tried lot of medical treatments and also prayed to all the Hindu gods but all in vain.

In the year 1976,on a Good Friday occasion, I took my daughter and went to attend the special service in Zion Gospel Prayer Fellowship Church of Sister Sarah Navaroji. After the meetings Sister Navaroji prayed to many people and prayed for my daughter also with tears bursting from her eyes. My daughter got complete healing from all her sickness and the child started walking. This miracle transformed me .I was born again and took immerse water baptism. According to Galatians 6:17 I preferred to take the marks of Jesus on my body and I removed all jewels that I was wearing to beautify myself. I was indeed very happy and rejoicing in the Lord and that nothing can separate me from the Love of Christ. But my husband did not like this change in me.

During this time, my husband was falsely accused in his office for the wrong doing of some one else by mistake and he was suspended from work. He was so much dejected that he bought some sleeping pills to commit suicide. So,I compelled my husband to come with me to Zion Gospel Prayer Fellowship Church and took him to the worship meeting one Sunday. After the meeting my husband said he was deeply touched by the song and the message of Sister Sarah Navaroji. Very next thing he did was that he went to a Bible exhibition and bought a Bible for him. After attending two Sunday services regularly, my husband took immerse baptism in water and also received the anointing of the Holy Spirit. Sister Navaroji prayed for us and prayed for the problem in his job. God did a miracle and my husband's suspension order was revoked clearing all the accusations. He joined his duty back by the grace of God.

In the year 1993, my husband while in office suffered a sudden stroke in which he was partially paralyzed. He was admitted in the hospital for treatment for some time. The whole church stood with us and prayed for him. Sister also prayed for him. After one year sick leave the Lord gave him strength to resume duty. Also he was promoted as 'District Revenue Officer' and was posted in Tiruchi. After some years we both took voluntary retirement and actively participating in the Church services. Praise the Lord!

Priscilla

b)   Brother   MASILAMANI   FAMILY   , Ambattur

(Superintendent, P.W.D, Chennai)
In the year 1973, I heard few songs of Sister Sarah Navaroji   in the Radio program. Songs like,
*'Inaiyilla Naamam' (meaning) 'The matchless Name' Song no.21.

   *'Thudhithu paadida paathirame'(meaning)'Worthy to sing Praises' Song no. 5.

have overwhelmed me with joy. I wanted to see her and listen to her

preaching well. Eventually I went to Z.G.P.F. Church. I felt the

presence of God in the Church worship Service. Week by week as
I started hearing the divine inspired Songs of Sister Navaroji and her deep messages, I began to taste the love of God, and there I was born again taking immerse water baptism. Since then the Lord has been doing many miracles to my family through Sister Sarah Navaroji's prayer.

In the year 1974 God healed me miraculously from Small Pox disease.
In the year 1981, the material and physical losses caused to our family due to the hatred of some people have all come to naught and God replenished us with a good house and lot of blessings.
In the year 1997 ,when my wife was bedridden due to severe hip disorder, Sister Navaroji came to our house personally and prayed. My wife got immediate relief.

Many more are the miracles the Lord is doing in our family ever since. Glory to God!

Masilamani

c) Sister ESTHER and her son SAMUEL (M..B.B.S.), Pondichery

I, Gangabai, Puduchery am from a staunch Hindu family background. My younger son namely Velmurugan was born with kidney disease on 1.4.1990. and had been battling for life. At the age of 13 his both kidneys stopped functioning. We landed up in Govt. General Hospital , Chennai for treatment. From the year 2003 to 2006 repeated surgeries were done. Finally, one of the kidney was to be transplanted from mother. Even after that he was struggling for life.

At that time, with all our relatives distancing themselves from us, perplexed , as I and my son were spending our time in the G.H ward without any future hope, one brother Jayakumar (Engineer, T.N.E.B.) from Zion Gospel Prayer Fellowship Church, visited us and prayed for us. Later he took us to the Church. Glory be to God!

Due to the continuous prayer of Sister Sarah Navaroji and her regular teaching and preaching from the Bible, Jesus healed my son.

We accepted Lord Jesus Christ as our Saviour and Lord God who continues to do miracles in our lives. I am now named Esther and my son Samuel. He, Samuel, is an M.B.B.S Student now who discontinued his study at 8th Standard due to his critical illness.

If Jesus can do this miracle to us, He can do it for you too. Would you believe!

All Praise to Jesus!

Esther

3.7.2 CHRISTIAN LEADERS TESTIMONY

Here are some Christian Leaders sharing from their heart and personal experience with the God given Chuch Ministry of Sister Sarah Navaroji.

a) Pastor. J. EDWIN RAJKUMAR & Mrs.GETSY EDWIN,
TAMIL FULL GOSPEL CHURCH (International), DUBAI.
Pastor J. Edwin Rajkumar.
I know Sister Sarah Navaroji from the year 1966. My younger Sister Eunice took training for Church Ministry Work in the year 1971 from Sister Sarah Navaroji. Since then I had close fellowship with Sister's Church and her Ministry. I am so grateful to her all through my life because she had chosen the right life partner for me and also conducted our marriage which was the first wedding in her Church.

Pastor.J.Edwin Mrs.Getsy Edwin

There is no limit for the love and affection Sister Sarah Navaroji has shown to our family. I had been inspired and blessed by all her ministries.

Today I am Pastoring a large congregation in Dubai. Once I invited her to Dubai to preach God's word to people in that area. People who all attended these special Revival meetings were so much blessed by Sister's divine inspired songs and anointed messages that they experienced the seasons of refreshing.
Glory to God!.

Pastor. J.Edwin Rajkumar

Mrs. Getsy Edwin
I know Sister Sarah Navaroji from my age of 13. In the year 1962 as a family we were worshipping in a small Church at Vepery along with Sister. During these days

Sister Navaroji has composed many melodious divine inspired songs. Some famous songs are,

'Enthan Anbulla Aandavar Yesuve'Song No.9 (meaning) 'My beloved Lord Jesus'
'Motsha yathirai selgiroam'Song No.178 (meaning) 'Heavenward journey we march'
'Jaya Kristhu munselgiraar'Song No.175 (meaning)'Christ the victorious goeth ahead'

Then she use to teach us to sing them in the Church.
She also prophetically told that the Lord has given her a vision that these songs will spread all over the world. Even though we did not believe it at that time but when H.M.V. establishment started recording Sister's songs, we realized that God is fulfilling the vision He gave her.
Sister Navaroji has chosen a right life partner for me and conducted our marriage in her Church.., which she established later. Ours is the first wedding in that Church.
Her exemplary Ministry enabled me to stand firm together with my husband to Pastor a big Church in Dubai.
All glory be to God !.

Mrs. Getsy Edwin

b) Brother Dr. R. STANLEY , B.E., M.Tech., D.D.
 Vellore
BIBLE TEACHER
Brother .R. Stanley was working as Construction Engineer in C.M.C. Hospital , Vellore. He is an architect by Profession who turned to be a Bible Teacher. He is also

an Evangelist, great missionary leader.

He established , 'Full Gospel Young Men/Women Association" having its centre in Vellore in the year 1971. Later the name of the organization was changed to , 'Blessing Youth Mission'.

Countless are the young men and women who have surrendered their lives to Jesus Christ and also dedicated for Missionary work.

Brother R. Stanley , during his M.Tech (Post Graduate Engineering) studies in I.I.T.,Madras use to attend Sunday Services of Zion Gospel Prayer Fellowship Church, Chennai regularly and listen to Sister Sarah Navaroji.s preaching of the word of God . The messages and songs of Sister Navaroji has created even more thirst and desire within him to win souls for the kingdom of God.

In the IIT Campus itself, he use to be canvassing his fellow students for the Kingdom of God. Almost every week in the Sunday worship service he would be seen sharing new new testimonies about the Lords work with him.

Even today he is preaching and teaching the word of God in T.V. and in Gospel Crusades.

Glory be to God !

c) Pastor OWAN ROBERTS, Chennai.

GOOD SAMARITAN FELLOWSHIP CHURCH, Hossanna Towers, Kodungaiyur

Pastor Owan Roberts was a great servant of God who has preached the Gospel of Jesus Christ all over the world. Countless are those who have been touched by the Lord through his powerful messages and healing gifts.

He has planted many Churches through , ' Good Samaritan Fellowship.' and in Chennai he has established a big Church congregation at Kodungaiyur.

During his youth days Pastor Owan Roberts use to regularly attend 'Zion Gospel Prayer Fellowship Church ' services of Sister Sarah Navaroji. After the Church service, straightaway he used to proceed for village ministries and street preaching.

The fiery ministry of Sister Sarah Navaroji has in a great deal encouraged and energized this well known missionary Leader and Pastor.

We Praise God for His wonderful work !

d) Pastor.A.PRATAPSINGH- Trinity Full Gospel Church, Chennai

I am so glad and happy to see the Life and Ministry of Sister Sarah Navaroji

has been published in a book form.

Ever since Sister has established the Zion Gospel Prayer Fellowship Church,

I had the opportunity to know about her and to take part in her ministries.

Like me, for those who know about the ministries of Sister Sarah Navaroji

 and the hardships she faced in all her works for the Lord, it would give

confidence that ' The Lord will take care. '

If I have to say which of her songs touched me, I have to sayall of them.

My warm greetings to Sister Lalitha Evangeline who is a close help in Sister Sarah Navaroji's ministries and to Rev. Dr. R. Samuel. who has wonderfully written and published this book.
May God give many more years of life to Sister Sarah Navaroji and continue to use her in his great ministry.   Glory to God !

Pastor.A.Pratap Singh

Superintending Pastor

e) Mrs. HEPHZIBAH PRATAPSINGH
TRINITY FULL GOSPEL CHURCH, Ayanavaram, Chennai 23.

Sister Sarah Navaroji is a chosen vessel of God . Her preaching and songs have been a great blessing to me. From the year 1967 to 1970 I had the opportunity to take part in the Sunday Services of Zion Gospel Prayer Fellowship Church led by Sister Sarah Navaroji. I have learnt the fear of God, spiritual thirst, victorious prayer life through Sister. They are even today precious to me. Next to God I am grateful to Sister Sarah Navaroji.

Mrs. Hephzibah
Pratapsingh

I use to regularly attend all the crusade meetings Sister hasconducted in S.I.A.A. grounds, Chennai. I use to write down clearly all

the messages she preaches there. When I go back to College in Coimbatore
where I was working, I use to read out those messages to my colleagues .
They have all testified that they were blessed by those messages.
 Moreover, I bought the LP records and Cassettes of Songs like,

'Um paatham paninthane' Song No.15 (meaning) 'I bow down thy feet'
'Nigare illatha Sarvesaa' Song No.20 (meaning) 'O! thou ! matchless Almighty'

and played it for them which were very much useful in their spiritual life. In the recent days also I use to buy Sister's Song CD's and gift them to many known persons.
Next to God, I owe her a good deal for my prayer life, Fear of God and Spiritual Thirst. Indeed, in a great measure has she contributed to the body of Christ!

Mrs Hephzibah Pratapsingh

3.8.1 An International Institute honouring Ministrial service(1986).
Sister Sarah Navaroji has been conferred with DOCTOR OF DIVINITY Degree for her contributions and excellence in the manifold ministries of the Lord (Song ministry, Preaching ministry, Prophetical ministry and Church Planting ministry) from the INTERNATIONAL INSTITUTE OF CHURCH MANAGEMENT, Rhode, Island, U.S.A. by Dr. John Williams, The Founder and President of this Institute.

3.8.2 Academy Award appreciating great Gospel works (2000).

Appreciating Sister Sarah Navaroji's far reaching Gospel proclaiming campaigns and crusades 'The World Tamil Christian Academy' functioning from Tambaram has awarded the title 'Good News Champian' called in Tamil (Narchadi Selvar) and glorified God.

3.9 Church Planting in Sub-Urbs

From the year 1972 to 1975 Sister Sarah Navaroji had gone around the sub-urbs of Madras(Chennai) city and proclaimed the Gospel. As a result of these ministries at a churches have been planted and church ministries are continuing in number of places and some of them are:-

a) Kamarajapuram (Seliyur)

b) Veppampattu

c) Vizhudumangalam

d) Thirumazhisai

Every Sunday brothers from the city church will go to these respective churches to conduct worship meetings and edify the believers. When Holy Communion and Baptism services are conducted in the City church all the believers from these Sub-Urb churches will attend to take part in the Lord's table.

3.10 Churches Planted in other Places

In the Crusades within India and abroad where ever Sister Sarah Navaroji has preached the Gospel, numerous souls were touched and have accepted Lord Jesus Christ as their personal Saviour. Due to this bountiful harvest, many churches have come up in various locations and are functioning on their own which are out of our record. Hence, it is difficult to list them here. However, we would like to mention about three important nearby locations.

3.10.1 MADURAI (THIRUMANGALAM) CHURCH

During the years from 1970 to 1972 Sister Navaroji had preached in a number of Gospel Meetings in and around Madurai upon the invitation of Christian Leaders of different denominations joined to-gether. As an outcome of her Crusades she planted a Church in Thirumangalam area and appointed a local leader to shepherd the Church.

HERE IS THE TESTIMONY.

a) Pastor. VICTOR SEENI.

CHRIST CHURCH, ZION GOSPEL PRAYER FELLOWSHIP,

Zion Nagar, Thirumangalam , Madurai.

During the year from 1970 to 1985, God's word was sown in this area by Sister Sarah Navaroji. Today we are reaping the harvest of the Living Words that were sown in those days.

Being inspired by the Holy Spirit, few of us believers took efforts to spread the Gospel of Lord Jesus Christ in this area through the ministry of Sister Sarah Navaroji.

After her first crusade in the year 1970, a Church was planted here and we named it Zion Gospel Prayer Fellowship Church in Thirumangalam.

People from Sivakasi , Virudunagar, Madurai, Usalampatti haved come, took part in the Crusade and were baptized in water. Once in a Revival Meeting at Thamukkam grounds, Madurai, Sister Sarah Navaroji made every one to kneel down and pray and many received the Baptism of the Holy Spirit.

The Lord enabled me to arrange these meetings and take part in all of them. Today in Thirumangalam , there is a small town called 'Zion Nagar'. Sister Sarah Navaroji planted a Church here, dedicated it and it is growing day by day.

I wish to share this testimony with much gratitude.

Praise the Lord!.

Pastor. Victor Seeni

b) Brother.THANGARAJ (L.I.C. Officer. Retd. Madurai)

In the year 1970 , I was fresh from my college education, desperately seeking for a job to support my big family due to the sudden demise of my father. We were pushed to the bottom of the poverty line.

It was at that time a branch of Zion Gospel Prayer Fellowship Church of Sister Sarah Navaroji was started afresh at Thirumangalam , Madurai with two families, that is, Victor Seeni and Williams both well known to me. My class teacher Mrs. Flora Williams and my Sisters class teacher Mrs. Diana Victor advised me to attend this Church.

The messages sent by Sister Sarah Navaroji were preached here every Sunday and Sisters soul stirring songs were sung. There anointed words comforted me and uplifted my family life. I turned to Christ. He did not disappoint me.

The songs that have comforted me in distress are,

'Kathiravan thondrum kaalai yidhe (meaning) 'Behold, the morning sunrise

Puthiya kirubai pozhindthiduthe' Song No.3   showers the mercy anew'

'Karthar anbae thooya anbe' Song No.134 (meaning)'Lord's Love, the pure Love'

If I were not drawn to Christ by the ministries of Sister Sarah Navaroji , either I would have committed suicide or run away from my family. I Praise the Lord Jesus for saving me!.

Thangaraj

3.10.2) TIRUCHY CHURCH

In Tiruchy area also during the years 1969 to 1973 Sister addressed number of Revival Meetings arranged by the Church leaders cutting across the barriers of denomination, those who had burden for souls. Two Pentecostal Churches were planted here by Sister and gave the Pastoral responsibility to two brothers namely Ponkalan and Santhanadan.
HERE IS THE TESTIMONY

Brother.Ponkalan

Our beloved Sister Sarah Navaroji Gods chosen vessel had ministered in many Gospel revival meetings. As a result there was a big harvest in this area. Large number of People accepted Jesus Christ and became born again Christians. Sister Planted New Pentecostal Church here. Pastor.Lazarus used to come every month and minister to us with Holy Communion and Baptism service. The Lord enabled to conduct a Sunday School Service for about 100 children. Hindu and Muslim children also use to join with us happily and learn Bible verses and Sister's composed songs. Brother.Aquila was then posted here in the Govt. Revenue department as D.R.O. He along with his wife Sister.Priscilla and Son Moses use to come and help us in this Sunday School Children ministry.

As the years went by the Lord gave the increase. More and more believers in the Church dedicated themselves for the full time Lords Service and started their own ministries in different places and planted churches wherever the Lord took them.

One brother R.Samuel has planted many churches in Coimbatore area and is ministering there.

Pastor. Philip in Pudhu vayal of Pudu Kottai, Pastor. Pauldoss in Thuvakudi now taken care by his son, Pastor. Sunder Singh in Banglore have planted churches in these respective areas. Also, Pastor.S.P Lazarus is now doing the 'Endrendrum Aanandam – Joy Forever' ministries from Kajapet, Trichy spreading all over surounding areas.by the grace of God.

While the Church planted initially in Tiruchy is not functioning now at that place, the ministry has spread across many areas and more number of churches have been planted down the years.

By Gods abundant grace for the past 40 years I and my son Robinson visit the Zion Gospel Prayer Fellowship Church in Chennai frequently and are blessed by the Ministry of Sister Sarah Navaroji till now. At one time Robinson met with an accident and suffered wounds in his face, hands and legs. We immediately called up Sister over phone for prayer. Sister prophetically told that Robinson will be healed and there will be no scar of the wound any where in his body.

It happened the same way. Glory to God!

3.10.3) RANIPET CHURCH

In the year 1974 Sister Navaroji was invited to preach in a Convention in Ranipet by some born again Christian beleivers.Eventually,a Church sprang up there by the anointed Gospel messages given by Sister. This Church has also been handed over to the local leaders and is functioning independently.

3.11 Training Workers for the Mission Field (1970 – 1979)

As the Lord said in Matthew 9:37 & 38

"The harvest is plentiful but the workers are few.

Ask the Lord to send out workers into his harvest field."

It was the deep longing and prayer of Sister that more workers to be sent in the mission field. So, she started a training camp for as many as 40 brothers and sisters to be trained in the mission work. It was started in the year 1970.Brothers were accommodated in another place and sisters were lodged in the same premises. They were trained for all necessary works required for Evangelism such as out door ministry, church ministry, preaching, teaching and serving the table etc., The training went on till 1979 and all who took training were able to go out and do ministry on their own or join various

other churches to continue their ministry as the Lord guided them.In the Bible we read that great leaders did not keep the work of God to themselves but trained others also in to the work..In the New Testament we see that Jesus trained 12 disciples and in turn

they trained many Apostles to be engaged in the Lords vineyard. Not only that ,but also the mission field is so vast and open, that it is not possible by one or two men and women to accomplish God's mission. More and more men and women should be

trained and prepared to be sent out and do evangelism in the nook and corner of all over the world. This great task of training and sending out workers into the Lord's harvest field, Sister has faithfully done during the years of 1970 to 1979.

However, the process of training mission workers continued in Sister's ministry so that many a leading Preachers and Pastors of to-day are an outcome to this.

Even as the work of the Lord is carried out mightily, the devil also works with his full strength. As we read in the scripture,

'Your adversary the devil, as a roaring lion, walketh about, seeking whom he may devour.' I Peter 5: 8

the devil did work in the missionary training camp creating internal conflicts.

Therefore Apostle Paul has warned in the same verse,

'be sober, be vigilant'

However, many out of their selfish motive give place to the devil without being vigilant in their ministry. Devil did use such people and tried to bring disrepute to Sister Sarah Navaroji and to the other co-workers. But , Jesus Christ the head and corner stone of the Church being King of kings and Lord of lords had sub-dued the devil and his subtle plans (Rev 17:14). The devil who wanted to give defeat had all his counsels foiled and according to the Romans 8:37 , in all these things fully victory was given through Christ who loved us.

The brothers and sisters who took training dispersed and gone to various places to do their ministry independently or by joining other churches as the Lord guided them.

'Therefore they that were scattered abroad went
every where preaching the word.' Acts 8:4
As this verse rightly says, such incidents take place in the
Church history time and again and resulted in growth of
the Church. Defeat to the devil and Victory to God's
people.
Jesus Christ in his report submitted to the Father about
concluding his ministry on the earth said in John 17:12,
'none of them is lost, but the son of perdition;
 that the scripture might be fulfilled.'
It is our firm belief that none who took part in the training
mission have been lost.

CHAPTER 4 -Crusade Ministries

Sister Sarah Navaroj Preaching5

Crusade Ministries

4.1 Introduction

"Therefore, go and make disciples of all nations, baptizing them in the name of the Father and of the Son and of the Holy Spirit, and teaching them to obey everything I have commanded you. And surely I am with you always." Mathew 28: 19,20.

This is the express command of Lord Jesus Christ himself to all disciples. Sister Sarah Navaroji did not confine herself inside her residence at Kilpauk, Madras to do her ministry. She knew the necessity and urgency to reach the unreached .Also she was constrained,urged and burdened by the Holy Spirit to move out to proclaim the good news of salvation through Jesus by singing, preaching and praying for all those masses to whom the Lord took her to. She was not only preaching that the salvation comes by accepting Jesus as their personal Saviour, but also she was very particular teaching them that to obey the commandments of Jesus Christ which is the real sign of a true believer. Furthermore, she insisted that every believer should take immerse water Baptism according to the Bible verse quoted above and enter into the covenated fulnesss of Christian life.

4.2 Resistance/ Opposition

The admonishing teachings of the full Gospel messages by Sister Sarah Navaroji were an irritation to those Christian leaders who go on soft pedaling messages preaching only the blessings from God and not teaching the necessity of obeying God's commandments. It was not an easy task preaching that Salvation is only through Jesus Christ but also to proclaim the Full Gospel message in Public platforms. She continued to face opposition for the ministry and even threat to her own life.

Nevertheless, the Lord who promised in the verse,

' lo, I am with you always, even unto the end of the world.' Mathew 28: 20

has been always present with Sister Sarah Navaroji where ever she went to spread the Good News and protected her from all dangers.

Resistance and opposition to her ministries came from various quarters, like, Christians, non- Christians, relatives, sorcerers (witch craft) etc.The reason to oppose also was diverse. They are like Spirits against Jesus Ministry, doctrinal differences, mere jealousy and an un-accepting attitude of a woman doing such an overwhelming ministry. But, Sister Navaroji by all means has weathered out all the forces set against her mission. She took the same defensive and offensive weapons that Paul took in II Corinthians 10: 4,

The weapons we fight with are not the weapons of this world. On contrary, they have divine power to demolish strong holds. We demolish arguments and every pretension that sets itself up against the knowledge of God, and we take captive every thought to make it obedient to Christ."

4.3 Power of God in the Mission field

While Sister's Song ministry and Church ministry were going on from her residence at 46-Kuttiappan 2nd Street, Kilpauk , Chennai -10, she also maintained a relentless missionary tour within and without India addressing various Crusades and Gospel campaigns.Sister Sarah conducted such Crusades and Campaigns for over 50 years in the period of 20th and 21st century and toiled as a pioneer Evangelist who caused the Revival to spread like a wild fire in India and Abroad.

In her crusades, she use to preach the Full Gospel of Jesus and also teach the songs she composed. Thus Sister Sarah Navaroji"s songs have become popular all over Tamil Nadu in all churches. From there the songs have spread all over the world. Sister Sarah Navaroji's songs were sung in Church Services, Prayer meetings and Gospel meetings without any denominational differences.The beauty is that the songs by itself proclaim the Gospel of Jesus. It is because almost all songs contain the message of salvation, holy life, blessings and the second coming of Jesus Christ. Sister Navaroji is not only an eminent singer but she is also a very good orator. People do listen to her sermons spell bound for two to three hours continuous and some times even more than that. She is also a great crowd puller. People gather in masses to her crusades and convention meetings.Such crusades and convention meetings are usually held in open grounds to accommodate the gathering crowd. After the end of the meetings people queue up to get prayed by her individually. Healing the sick, casting out evil spirits, giving prophetic words are part of her crusade ministry.

The secret behind such a mighty deeds of the Lord in her Gospel Campaigns is that ,several days before the crusade meetings she use to spend lot of time in fasting and prayer. Also a group of believers, including her relatives pray together for the release of Gods power in the meetings. Sister Navaroji use to take regular fasting and prayer sessions and some times it has gone upto 40 days and even 80days. She does this before launching into specific ministry or while seeking guidance of the Holy Spirit for the future course of action in her mission.

4.4 Close Associates in the Ministry

As Sister Navaroji started her ministry from her residence at Kilpauk, Chennai , invitations started pouring in requesting her to come and preach in the Gospel meetings from all over Tamil Nadu and from other States of India. After some years she received invitations from other Countries as well.

Apart from the crusades others have invited Sister Sarah Navaroji to minister, She herself has organized regular crusades in Chennai (Madras) along with a group of believers who supported her ministry. Many individuals and families who accepted Jesus through these crusades have become members of her church in Kilpauk to be planted and rooted for generations. In all Sister's ministry there has been a small group of dedicated believers who extended their physical and prayer supports.

Even as Joshua says in Joshua 24: 15

" But as for me and my house, we will serve the Lord."

 has been true with Sister Sarah Navaroji.

From the very onset of her ministry, Sister Navaroji's mother Soundaram Asirvatham was always behind her providing time to time advise and encouragement. She even use to sit with her when visitors come and meet her.

Her elder Sister Lalitha Evangeline Jayakar along with her husband Brother Jayakar have rendered a great support in all organizing activities such as, works with printing press for song books, wall posters and hand bills for conventions. Co-coordinating with people who invite Sister for the meetings, taking care of visitors, arranging song recording activities and distribution of recorded cassettes and so on.

4.5 Steadfast mind in the Vision

Though the mission was a team work, Sister Sarah Navaroji was very careful about the vision that was given to her by the Lord and never let any one else deviate her attention from accomplishing the vision and call. In the long missionary journey many have joined her and many have left her according to one's own convenience or according to one's own call in the ministry but nothing deterred Sister Navaroji from what Apostle Paul says in

Philippians 3: 12

"I press on to take hold of that for which Christ Jesus took hold of me."

4.6 CRUSADES IN INDIA

As mentioned earlier Sister Sarah Navaroji along with her mother Soundaran Asirvatham settled in Chennai(Madras) at Kilpauk area after returning from Ceylon in1962.Even as she was conducting a small prayer meeting in her residence, the Holy Spirit started moving her to go out and preach the good news outside Madras to various places. Sister Navaroji had to launch her Gospel Campaign journey from the very same year 1962 without any lapse of time. Her crusade ministries all over India and abroad had to be done in parallel with her other ministries like Church ministry and Song ministry which had been epicentred at Kilpauk, Chennai(Madras). As the Scripture says in

Ephesians 5: 16 'Redeeming the time, because the days are evil'

the evil works of the devil is rampant in these last days. As each day passes by multitude of souls are perishing in sin without knowing the salvation through Jesus Christ and getting denied with the privilege of inheriting heaven. Therefore, realizing the need to utilize every minute without loosing any more time Sister Sarah expedited her outreach programs.

The Gospel Campaign tour of Sister Sarah Navaroji in India is described here in chronological order of year and places from the year 1962 to the maximum possible accuracy as far as the historical information are preserved and available.

4.6.1 Chennai City (Madras)

1. SAIDAPET , MADRAS (1962)

Upon starting her small level ministry as a prayer meeting in Kilpauk, Madras ,Sister Sarah Navaroji became known to the servants of God in Madras and around as a chosen vessel of the Lord. Pastor.N.Jeevanadam a well known anointed Servant of God invited Sister to preach in a three days convention meeting in a Church at Saidapet. But, before proceeding to Saidapet to speak in the Convention ,Sister Navaroji became very sick. Every one was worried how She could do this ministry. She had high fever in the sick bed even to the point of death. In that condition of deteriorating health she developed a deep desire to go to be with the Lord.Out of that intense longing within, a wonderful song emerged from her heart which she instantly composed and sang. Here is that marvelous poem:-

" Aanandamai inbakkannan yeagiduvein

Thooyappithavin   mugam   dharisippane."   Song No.28-Christian Songs of Joy Song book

(meaning)

" Joyfully shall I inherit the pleasant Canaan

And behold the face of Holy Father."

However, she immediately made up her mind remembering God's call in the ministry and realizing that it was only a starting point of her race, and prayed that the Lord should give strength to enable her to go to Saidapet and proclaim the Gospel. The heavenly Father gave her full strength to go and preach the word of God in the Saidapet Church convention. During that meeting, the same healing Power of the Lord that healed her has healed many sick people miraculously through her prayers. At the end many people surrendered their lives to Jesus.

2.ALLELUAH GROUNDS,Kilpauk ,Madras (1967, 1968)

It has been described earlier that in the year 1962, Sister Sarah Navaroji along with her mother settled in a house at Kilpauk area after returning from Ceylon.The small prayer meeting that she started here became a prayer fellowship and soon started functioning as a Church with very few families and individuals. At this point of time, Sister felt the necessity of holding a public Gospel meeting in that same area to proclaim the Salvation message of Jesus so that more people can hear and know Jesus.

In the year 1967 (July) and 1968 (May) Sister Navaroji conducted public Gospel meetings in the open venue called Alleluah ground opposite to the Kilpauk E.S.I hospital for continuous 10 days each year and preached powerful word of God from a temporarily erected stage. She also taught the anointed songs that she composed. Prophecies were pronounced by the guidance of the Holy Spirit. The whole ground was lit by tube lights and adequate P.A system was in place. Great crowd of people from near by area like Ayanavaram, Pursaiwalkam, Kilpauk and also from far distances came and witnessed the demonstration of the Power of the Holy Spirit in the grounds. Participants in the meeting also include passerby, onlookers and casual visitors.

God worked many miracles in these meetings. Many devil possessed people were delivered, sick healed and sinners turned to Jesus confessing their sins and accepting Jesus as their personal Saviour. Hundreds of people took immerse baptism in water and received the anointing of the Holy spirit. Many families and individuals thus saved joined the

Zion Gospel Prayer Fellowship Church here. Pastor.Maharaja Prasangiar and Pastor. N.Jeevanandam have rendered immense support and help for these meetings.
HERE IS JUST ONE WONDERFUL TESTIMONY

a) Pastor. P.S. RAJAN . B.Th., D.I.E
I was born in a Hindu family . I am the fourth child for my parents. My father expired when I was a child. Subsequently, my two elder brothers also died one after the other. Only my elder sister and I survived for my mother. So, my mother was very affectionate towards me. With much hardship she educated me up to high school (S.S.L.C.) studies.

The Storm in my life
All of a sudden I was attacked by a number of evil spirits. They tormented me day and night not allowing me to sleep . I used to cry aloud at the middle of the night.
When I got employed in Government Services like Civil Supplies Dept. and Railways, the evil spirits disturbance was so much, that I could not continue my job. My mother brought many enchanters who tried to relieve me from the clutches of devils. But they could not.
Finally, I decided to commit suicide. I left my house , my town and came to Chennai. One day as I was walking through the streets of Chennai aimlessly , I came to a place near Ayanavaram called Kilpauk. There Sister Sarah Navaroji was conducting a huge public Gospel. Meeting. I came to that ground as an onlooker. Suddenly, Sister uttered some prophetical words about me. She said.,
" O Hindu Brother , don't end your life. I am Jesus. I will

deliver you'.

After this many things took place,. I went to Zion Gospel Prayer Fellowship Church. There upon Sister Sarah Navaroji's counsel I took immersion Baptism in water. The evil spirits departed me . My Lord Jesus filled me with His Holy Spirit.

Sister Sarah Navaroji told me prophetically that Jesus is calling me for the full time ministry .   I obeyed God's call.

Today I am Pastoring in a big Church in Andhra Pradesh and serving my Lord Jesus.

Praise be unto the Name of the Lord Jesus.!

Pastor P.S.Rajan.

3. KILPAUK GARDEN ROAD,Madras (1968)

In the year 1968,Pastor.Samuel Daniel well known for Tracts ministry of Indian Christian Church at Kilpauk Garden Road (near to Sister's Church), arranged a special Gospel meeting and requested Sister to preach in that meeting. The gathered people were refreshed in spirit through the divine inspired songs and messages of Sister. Pastor.Maharaja also assisted her in these meetings.

4. S.I.A.A GROUND (Near Moore Market), Madras – (1969 – 1975)

After conducting the Public Gospel meetings in the open ground in the same locality(Kilpauk) where she had the church and witnessing the harvest the Lord gave, Sister Navaroji felt the necessity to enlarge the area of her ministry in Madras and had a burden that whole of the Madras should hear the Gospel of Jesus. So she found that the S.I.A.A ground near Madras Central Railway Station adjacent to the Moore Market being a center location as a suitable place to launch her crusade for Madras(Chennai).This location was,

A place where all buses and trains will come to Madras from all over Tamil nadu and even other states.
It was close to where Sister's Church is located (Kilpauk).
A public spot where always (day and night) lots of people are present.

Sister Navaroji prayed for it and upon the confirmation from the Holy Spirit decided to hold Gospel meetings in this ground in the year 1969. Starting from 1969 up to 1975 for seven years, every year in the month of May or June for 7 to 10 days continuously Sister conducted a massive crusade meetings here. All the believers of her church extended their helping hand to Sister for this great task.
Hand bills and wall posters were printed. Wall posters were pasted in every nook and corner and hand bills distributed all around Madras. Hand bills were also sent to many known people outside Madras. News paper advertisements were given.
As it is written in the Bible,
'...... youngmen/women, because you are strong, and the word of God abides in you, and you have overcome the wicked one.' I John 2:14
Sister Navaroji in her prime youth,early thirties, full of physical and spiritual vigour has preached powerful sermons from the word of God in all the meetings.The heavens were opened and the mighty Power of God descended and took control of the whole ground.

From the Podium She also sang the divine inspired songs composed by her with the group of other sisters. She utilized that opportunity to teach people to learn the tune and words so that they can keep singing these songs and enjoy the presence of God where ever they are. These power packed songs have floated in the air and traveled to far distances and touched many people in need and distress. Such people received instant relief, conviction and surrendered their lives to Jesus. People in train and buses were singing the songs of Jesus what they learnt in the meeting while returning.

The response for these meetings were tremendous and the results were overwhelming great crowd of people turned up to hear the songs and messages of Sister everyday. Christian leaders, Christian believers, non- Christians who have come to attend these meetings from far and near by distances as families and as individuals, passers by, on lookers and such were the mixed crowd of audience gathered.The geographical location chosen for this historical crusade was befitting for all practical purposes. It was a central place of Madras with convenient transport arrangements of those days Madras and also a near by place to Sisters church location in Kilpauk. The Lord has shown immense grace for these meetings. They were the first of its kind in those years. The Power of God was released abundantly and people received showers of blessings.The Gospel Meetings Conducted by Sister Sarah Navaroji in S.I.A.A ground was a Record Break from any other Christian Meetings conducted in those days and that too by an individual woman missionary. All glory and honour to God alone.

Oppositions not excluded

Oppositions were also there including witch crafting. One man who was living near by S.I.A.A ground started distributing hand bills against Sister accusing her of calling people as sinners. He was even found scolding and shouting Sister publicly inspite of people in the crowd preventing him.He gave a death threat also. But within few days the man started vomiting blood in his house and his wife came to Sister begging her to pray for her husband. But the man died of severe blood vomiting. In another incident while everyone in the church premises were out gone for these meetings, a robber

entered the building to steal something. But while he was on the terrace of the building he got appendices pain and could not move further so that he needed to be carried to hospital by others

The Secret of success

We read in the Bible Mathew 4th Chapter that Jesus Christ before starting his ministry spent 40 days in fasting and prayer. As a faithful disciple following the Master, Sister Sarah use to take 40 days fasting and pray before each year S.I.A.A ground crusades. Also a week before the meetings commence, Sister Navaroji and her elder Sister Lalitha with her family and somebelievers of the church use to walk around the S.I.A.A ground once everyday for six days and seven times on the seventh day that is the starting day of the meeting with praising and praying in order to conquer the area. This they did as the symbolic performance of what God commanded Israelites to do when they conquered Jericho.

Further more, even as Sister Navaroji use to go up on the dias to preach the word of God a group of Sisters gather behind the stage in a small tent and keep praying. The

Power of this prayer use to be demonstrated in the ground as the powerful word of God and the anointed songs gush out from the Servant of God's mouth.

At the end of the meetings it could be noticed that crowd of people rush to come forward accepting Jesus as their Lord and God.Many who were at the verge of death and heading towards committing suicide were pulled back to taste the love of God and found abundant life in Jesus Christ. Many people who were worshippers of idols and vain gods found the true God to worship in truth and spirit. Many people who were making a meaningless effort in search of mukthi found a meaning full eternal life with Jesus the saviour.Further more, many people who were suffering from various problems in life like over burdened debts, quarrels in family, placeless daily life, evil spirit haunting, troubles due to witch craft,uncurable diseases were all touched by the nail pierced hands of Jesus and delivered to be redeemed by His precious blood shed for them on the cross. Such redeemed people took immerse baptism in water in masses. Out pouring of the Holy Spirit on many born-again Christians were witnessed. Many families and individuals saved through these meetings have joined the Zion Gospel Prayer Fellowship Church founded by Sister Sarah Navaroji.

There were also many who came forward dedicating themselves for the full time ministry of of the Lord. Out of them nearly 40 brothers and sisters were given Missionary Training in Zion Gospel Prayer Fellowship Church from 1970 to 1979 about which it has been mentioned in the previous chapters. From those who took training, there are leading Pastors in C.P.M and other Churches to-day. Some others have gone out to start their own ministry as

Evangelists, Preachers and Pastors. We keep hearing about the wonderful ministry these beloved Servants of God are doing in their regions.

WITNESSES

WE WISH TO PRESENT A FEW TESTIMONIES FROM THE GREAT CLOUD OF WITNESSES HARVESTED IN THE HISTORICAL S.I.A.A GROUNG CRUSADES.

a) Brother.SPENCER WATTS

I was born in Kerala in a nominal Christian family and my parents use to take me to CSI church.

I was a nominal Christian . Adding to this, one of my uncle taught me that there in no God and The Bible is not true. I believed his words and that extinguished even the little bit of faith I had in God.

After my graduation I got a job. Practically I had everything I wanted. But deep within my heart, I felt a vacuum and a fear of death. At that juncture, two of my friends invited me to come with them for a crusade where Sister.Sarah Navaroji was preaching Gods word with melodious songs. So, I went with them to attend that crusade meetings.

It was in S.I.A.A Grounds near Moore market adjacent to Madras Central Station that Sister.Sarah Navaroji was conducting this Gospel meetings. Earlier I had attended some crusades where there use to be a lot of music and show. But this was totally different.There was nothing on the stage except a table with white cloth spread on it. At 6.30 p.m Sister Sarah Navaroji came to deliver Gods word. She first began to pray by singing a song ' O river of God'.

There was pin drop silence all over and a solemn calmness prevailed in the ground even though it is among the busy place of Madras. The presence of God was visibly felt by every one in the crowd attending the meeting. Sister Navaroji gave message from I Corinthians 1:18

"For the message of the cross is foolishness to those who are perishing, but to us who are being saved it is the power of God.

Sister also spoke about the nation Israel. She said in her message that the Second coming of Lord Jesus Christ is very near. If we are not washed by his precious blood and be saved we cannot get to the Kingdom of God. I saw a mighty out pouring of the Holy Spirit there in the ground. I was deeply touched by the personal testimony of Sister Navaroji. When I went back to my room, I wept very bitterly for my sins and asked the Lord to forgive me. A heavenly joy and peace filled my heart and that day I was born again

After the experience of personal Salvation, I was regularly attending Zion Gospel Prayer Fellowship Church founded by Sister Sarah Navaroji at Kuttiappan Street, Kilpauk, Chennai. With great hunger and thirst I was reading the Bible regularly and also with a deep burden I started sharing the Gospel to others.

I was working for M/S Lawrence & Mayo in Madras (Chennai) for 23 years and served the organization faithfully. Suddenly, I was falsely accused for some offences that I have not committed and the management abruptly removed me from job. This was a sudden shock to me. However, Jesus never failed. When I prayed the good Lord has provided me another good job to meet my needs. Presently I am working for a Christian Organization as an Accountant. Every day the Lord teaches me something new and keeps me going forward in the ministry.

I am an elder in the Church and serving the Lord faithfully in the capacity in which he has called me.

All Praise and honor be unto Him and Him alone.

Spencer Watts

b) Sister. GLORY EDWARD, Chennai

I was born and brought up in a good C.S.I. Christian family. However I did not have the born again Christian experience and the New Life through Lord Jesus Christ.

Glory Edward

Also from my child hood I was suffering from Chronic headache. My mother tried with many doctors but I could not be healed. My elder Sister Joice Elizabeth who was a member of 'ZION GOSPEL PRAYERFELLOWSHIP CHURCH', Chennai, lead by Sister Sarah Navaroji , took me to the Revival Crusade conducted by Sister Navaroji at S.I.A.A grounds, Chennai in the year 1969. There in the meeting Sister Sarah Navaroji prophetically told about me and immediately I felt a relief from my chronic disease. Also I surrendered my life to Jesus and instantly I was filled with the Holy Spirit. Later as a family I joined ZGPF church. The Lord continues to do miracles to our family both for our physical and spiritual needs.

Praise be to Jesus Name!

Glory Edward

c) Sister.VICTORIA JEBASUNDARY, Chennai

I was born in a pious Christian family but had been ignorant about the eternal life and blessings of New life in Lord Jesus Christ as written in the Holy Bible.

I had the opportunity to attend the S.I.A.A. grounds, Chennai Crusade.
The soul stirring songs and powerful messages delivered by
Sister Sarah Navaroji changed my life. I was born again, baptized by immersion in water and joined Z.G.P.F. Church.
In the year 1985, I suffered a severe Electric Shock. I could not move my hands and one portion of leg also became numb. By Sister Navaroji's prayer in a Good Friday Service God completely healed me. Many more are the miracles the Lord is doing for me since then!
Praise the Lord !

Victoria Jebasundary

d) Brother.M.FRANKLYN, Pallavaram, Chennai
    Manager, South Sales, M.S.Graphics Ltd.,Chennai

I was born and brought up in a Roman Catholic Christian family, strictly adhering to all religious formalities, but we did not like people preaching and teaching the Gospel according to The Bible.

In the year 1974, when our family was in a dire need of help, all doors were shut in front
of us. At that crucial time, in the month of May 1974,my mother Theresa heard about the Gospel crusade Sister.

Sarah Navaroji was conducting at S.I.A.A grounds, Chennai. My mother, my father along with mother's elder Sister and elder brother attended the Crusade meeting. All were so much comforted by the Word of God preached by Sister.Sarah Navaroji in that public meeting and also were deeply touched by the melodious and soul stirring songs she sang.

Subsequently, all the three families together went to Zion Gospel Prayer Fellowship Church, became members by taking immerse water Baptism according to the commandment of God in the Bible. In fact, Sister Sarah Navaroji being prompted by the Holy Spirit had prayed that the Lord should bring three Roman Catholic families that year,1974, to the true faith. The prayer was thus answered.

There after the good Lord met all our needs and started blessing us materially and spiritually. All the children got good education, well placed job and timely marriages. We are now living happily in the Lord.

Sister Navaroji gave a new Name to my mother calling 'GLORY SAMADANAM'. One day when Sister Sarah Navaroji was composing one of the famous song, Song No.324

'Pilavunda malayinullae – Deva   (meaning)   'within the cleft of rock

 Prasannathil naan Vazhgiren   live I
in the presence of God

Magimai   samadanam   perannandamae
     Glory, peace and great joy

Mannan maligaiyil en pidha veetylae   in my
father's house – the king's mansion
the Lord revealed to her the death of my mother. Even as

Sister Navaroji was in a state of shock and asked the Lord not to take away this beloved sister who is so useful in the ministry ,she received a phone call from our home informing her that my mother passed away to be with the Lord. The good Lord said to Sister ' my beloved daughter has finished her race and entered the glory and peace in my home as you gave her a new name GLORY SAMADANAM.' Sister Sarah Navaroji came to our house and conducted the funeral service herself and taught us this song there.

Praise be to the Name of Lord Jesus Christ. Amen!

M.Franklyn

5. SEERANI ARANGAM(STADIUM)-Marina Beach, Chennai. (1988-12th to 14th May)

Church of God , Kilpauk branch, Chennai has arranged for a massive Gospel crusade in the year 1988 at Marnia Beach, Seerani Stadium, Chennai.. Pastor. Wellesly Solomon, the then Pastor –in- Charge of Church of God and all the elders of the Church have made all the arrangements for this meeting. They have invited Sister Sarah Navaroji to preach the Good News in all the 3 days meetings from 12 th to 14th of May, 1988

People from Chennai and also from other parts of Tamil Nadu who heard that Sister Sarah Navaroji is going to Address a revival meeting in Chennai after a gap of many years have gathered in large numbers to listen to her power packed messages and melodious songs. The Lord commanded a big harvest. Many souls saved in these meetings were taken onboard by the Church of God co-workers and were nurtured in their spiritual life.

Also people who were touched by the anointed songs together with the Gospel preached of Sister Navaroji and

got deliverance from their life problems have visited Zion Gospel Prayer Fellowship Church as individuals and families.They were born again and became continued memebers of the Church till today.
ONE SUCH WITNESS WE WANT TO PRESENT HERE
a) Brother.A. JAYA KUMAR JOHN DANIEL , Assistant Executive Engineer, TNEB

I was born on the 14th day of August 1958 at Jolarpet, North Arcot Dist., to a good Christian Parents from C.S.I Church. I did my Diploma in Electrical Engineering from CPT, Adyar, Chennai. Immediately after finishing my Diploma I got Govt job and joined TNEB near Arakkonam (Mosur) as an Operator. Though I was born to a good Christian Parents I did not know the Lord Jesus Christ as my personal Saviour till the age of 29. Till then I was leading a life as we read in Ephesians 4:22 " ....your former way of life,......... your old self life, which is being corrupted by its deceitful desires;".
During my School days, I fell down while playing foot ball and had a severe knee joint dislocation on the right leg.I was treated at the famous traditional bone healers at Puthur. However, I use to get the disloctation problem every now and then and had to be treated everytime. Again, during my Diploma studies, I met with a road accident and suffered from head injury. I was in coma stage for 4 days. When I got conscious ,I found my left eye lost 50% of sight. In Govt. General Hospital a scanning check was taken and they detected blood clot. Doctors gave medicine to dissolve the blood clot. I also started suffering from asthma due to which it was difficult to

breath specially at night time. These early age sickness continued even after my married life and tormented me. I thought that I will never have relief and so decided to commit suicide. I tried several times to commit suicide but the good Lord Jesus Christ protected me from all those attempts because he chose me before the foundation of this world for him as we read in Ephesians 1:4

"For he chose us in him before the creation of the world to be Holy… in his sight."

In the year 1981, I got married. My physcical ailments continued.

In the year 1988, Sister Sarah Navaroji was preaching in a large Crusade meeting being conducted at the Marina beach. I attended that meetings.The messages and the songs of Sister Sarah Navaroji attracted me. The Bible verse that she quoted in her message from I Thessalonians 4:7

'For God did not call us to uncleanness, but unto holiness' has deeply touched me and since then I made some new decisions in my life. I started attending the Zion Gospel Prayer Fellowship Church of Sister Sarah Navaroji and was hearing her message every week.

I understood about the truth regarding immerse Baptism in water and on 9th October 1988, I obeyed God's command and took immerse Baptism in water given to me by Pastor.Lazarus who visits this church coming from Mathur, K.K Dist. Sister also prayed for my physcical ailments I was suffering all these years. The Lord healed me from all the disorders in my body and I am relieved of all pains.Since then I am continuously attending the Zion Gospel Prayer Fellowship Church and also actively participating in all out reach ministries through the church.

On 15th may 1989 I joined in Cheyyar as Junior Engineer on promotion.I served in Cheyyar for 11years by the grace of God .The Lord did many miracles in the work spot. As my workers carry out work in the live electric poles, many times they met with deadly accidents and the Lord gave them life through my prayers. I always insisted that none of my staff should take any kind of gift from any of our customers. It was a great witness in the work spot for the glory of the Lord.

I am working not only as an Engineer of TNEB but also as a Gospel Missionary of Jesus Christ. In my work spot and in other places I freely distribute tracts and share the good news of Salvation through Jesus Christ. I participate in the village ministries, hospital ministries, prison ministries along with other brothers of the Church.

May all the Praise, honour and glory be to the Father , Son and the Holy Spirit. Amen.

A. Jayakumar John Daniel

6. PERIYAR THIDAL (GROUNDS), Chennai. (1988, 31st May to 2nd June)

Soon after the massive crusade in Marina Beech ended, upon many people requests and by the guidance of the Holy Spirit Sister Sarah Navaroji has conducted another session of Gospel meetings in Periyar Thidal a closed ground which is at a nearby proximity of her Church.

People of Chennai and nearby areas experienced the seasons of refreasing in the Lord.

7. Y.M.C.A , NANDANAM, Chennai. (July 2001)

In the year 2001, a dear Sister in the Lord, Advocate. Christina ,had arranged a Gospel Meet in the Y.M.C.A Premises at Nandanam, Chennai and requested Sister

Sarah Navaroji to address the gathering. Even though the gathering was arranged for Youths, people of all age group arrived to hear the Songs and Speech of Sister Navaroji in that camp. All those who came returned with much blessings from the Lord.

4.6.2 Sub- Urban areas around Chennai (1972 – 2000)

' The time is fulfilled, and the kingdom of God is at hand: repent ye, and believe the Gospel' Mark 1:15

2000 years after Jesus proclaimed this Gospel, now the kingdom of God is even more nearer. Hence, Sister Sarah Navaroji had to accelerate her Gospel campaigns and this time she marched forward into the Sub-Urban areas of Chennai and there she exhorted and admonished people to come out from their sinful lives, idolatary, false belief,worship to evil spirits,witch craft, drunkenness and all kinds of evil and believe the only Holy God Lord Jesus Christ to become heirs for the Kingdom of God ,the heaven. Many Christian believers who heard the powerful pure discourses of Sister Sarah Navaroji in the Public platforms requested her to come to their towns also and preach the word of God. All those who invited her have arranged for Gospel revival meetings in their areas.

1 . VELACHERI (1963, 2000)

In the year 1963, the Pastor of the Advent Mission Church in Velacheri invited Sister to preach in their annual convention meeting. Due to Sister's Full Gospel message the church further got strengthened and more souls were added to the Lord's folk. Again in the year 2000 Sister addressed the Perinba Peruviza Crusade in Velacheri. The Lord of harvest granted yet another reaping of friuts.

'...from Jerusalem, and round about unto Illyricum, I have fully preached the Gospel of Christ' Romans 15:19

As Apostle Paul had said the above statement, so also Sister Sarah Navaroji had determined to preach the Gospel from Chennai (Madras) to all round about towns, cities, states and every where the full Gospel of Christ.

TAMBARAM (1972)

In the year 1972 in Kamarajapuram near Tambaram few devoted believers have arranged for a Gospel meeting in which Sister proclaimed the Gospel. As a result of this meeting a new Pentecostal Church was planted there. In the year 1992, Pastor.Nelson Varghese of International Christian Church invited Sister to speak in their convention.

THIRUMALIZAI, VILUDUMANGALAM & VEPPAMPATTU (1970)

These are some of the areas where the local believers have arranged Gospel meetings
where Sister ministered during 1970s. All theses places she has planted new Churches
which are functioning independantly by the local leaders under the guidance of elders from Zion Gospel Prayer Fellowship Church.

AVADI (1970)

Believers from Military Quarters have organized Gospel meeting in 1970 which has witnessed good revival and new people accepted Jesus as their saviour.

4.6.3 Major Towns and Cities near Chennai (1969 – 2000)

1. ARAKKONAM – (1969 , 2000)

Arakkonam an important junction of Train and Bus traffic had been visited by Sister Navaroji first in the year 1969 to preach in the C.S.I Convention meeting. Again in the year 2000, Pastor R.Joseph of a Full Gospel Church invited Sister to preach in the 4th Annual convention meeting.

2. KANCHIPURAM - (1980, 1985)

One of the Hindu temples strong hold has also been penetrated by the Gospel messages of Sister. In the year 1980 and 1985 Pastor.Nesayyan who was the first one to establish a Pentecostal Church in this Hindu idol fort has invited Sister Navaroji to speak in their annual convention meeting arranged in the Municipal High School ground. Members of all churches were invited. It was a season of refreashing.New believers were added to the Church.

3. CHENGALPATTU (1983)

In the year 1983 Sister visited Chengalpattu to preach in a Revival meeting. All church members took part. It was the largest gathering Chengalpattu has ever witnessed for a Gospel meeting in those years.

VELLORE (1974, 1980)

Pastor. Nellaiah of a Pentecostal Church in Vellore invited Sister to speak in their church annual Convention meeting in the year 1974 and 1980.Again in the year 2000 Pastor.Emmanual of Zion Pentecostal Church invited Sister and arranged the crusade in Kottai Maidanam.The large gathering who attended and listened to Sisters Songs and messages were spiritually refreshed.

RANIPET (1974)

In the year 1974 Sister visited Ranipet for a Gospel meeting. As a result of this ministry a new Church was founded in Ranipet.

4.6.4 Important Districts of Tamil Nadu

1. TIRUNELVELI AREA (1962- 1965)

As it is said earlier even as Sister started her ministry in Kilpauk, Madras in a very small scale, the Holy Spirit started moving her to go out of Madras to Preach the Gospel. To facilitate fulfilling His purpose God sent one Pastor.Maharaja Prasangiar to Sister. He invited her to come and preach the good news in Tirunelveli area. He arranged for Sister Navaroji to preach the word of God in the C.S.I Church annual conventions. Sister preached stressing on the importance of immerse water Baptism for the born again experience and the Holy Spirit anointing for the victorious life of every believer. Many Christians and non-Christians accepted took immerse baptism in water and received Holy Spirit anointing.

2. KANYA KUMARI DISTRICT (1965 – 1990)

From the year 1965 sister received many invitations from Kanya Kumari district the southern tip of India. Initially, she preached in a number of CSI Church annual conventions and later many Pentecostal churches arranged Revival meetings where Sister delivered the Full Gospel message. Sister's visit to Kanya Kumari district continued even upto 1990. Till to-day a lot of people from around the world who have received Spiritual enlightenment through Sister's ministry in K.K district keep calling to express their gratitude for all the blessings they are enjoying from the Lord.

During this period of her tour in K.K district, Pastor. J.Lazer met Sister and invited her to come and preach in the annual convention of his church in Mathur .From then on Sister was visiting the Mathur church to speak in their annual convention every year during the month of January.This association resulted in Pastor.Lazer visiting the Zion Gospel Prayer Fellowship Church in Madras every month on first Sundays to conduct the Holy Communion and Baptism services.

3. NAGAPATTINAM, ATTUR & KARUNGAL (1967,1970)

In the year 1967 and 1970 Sister toured in some important places like Nagapattinam, Attur and Karungal of which some are Christian hub. Rev.Gnanadikkam invited Sister to Nagapttinam to speak in the C.S.I Church Convention. In Attur also she preached in the C.S.I Convention invited by Rev. John. In Karungal Sister visited first in 1967 to preach in CSI convention and again in 1970 in Poonthoppu of Karungal Rev.S. Selvanayagam has invited Sister to speak in another CSI Convention. People from Trinelveli use to come in buses to attend these conventions.

The Lord showered former rain and later rain (spiritual rains) in these areas due to the repeated church conventions in which Sister Sarah preached God's word. As a result the Children of God from the C.S.I Church back ground learnt the Full Gospel and it became a turning point in their lives. These revival meetings have laid a foundation to fulfill God's plan to raise many a faithful missionaries from the C.S.I church families and accomplish His mighty deeds in the following years of time.

4.TUTICORIN, PALAYAMKOTTAI, NAZERETH (Pillayanmanai) (1967, 1970)

" for I will pour water upon him that is thirsty, and floods upon the dry ground: I will pour my spirit upon thy seed, and my blessing upon thine offspring:" Isaiah 44:3

As the Lord spoke through Prophet Isaiah in the above Bible verses, God was willing to pour the water of His word upon the people who were hungry to hear. In the years from 1967 to 1970 God sent His chosen vessel Sister Sarah Navaroji in these areas which are in the southern part of Tamil Nadu to pour His Spirit upon the God's people of Christian families. God made the rivers of living waters flow into the dry hearts of those who have not heard the Full Gospel of Jesus Christ.People who have not known the love of God and Salvation through Jesus have heard the Gospel of Christ and enmass took immerse Water Baptism dedicating their lives to Lord Jesus Christ.

Rev. Diraviyam Yesudasan invited Sister to Palayamkottai. Sister delivered Gods messages from the word of God and the CSI churches heard the full Gospel in accordance with the apostles doctrine.

In 1970,through the I.P.C Church Pastor. Mathias all churches joined together and invited Sister for a Gospel meeting in Tutikorin because they witnessed the mighty acts of the Lord in all her meetings. In the year 1988 Pastor.S.Chellappa invited Sister for a Good News festival meeting to Palayankottai. God met many people through her prophetical words.

5.MARTHANDAM   (Kanchirapuram   ),
VELLALANVELAI (K.K.Dist.)
DISAYANVELAI (Tirunelveli Dist)- (1967, 1968)

"How beautiful upon the mountains are the feet of him that bringeth good tidings,that publisheth peace;that bringeth good tidings of good,that publisheth salvation; saith unto Zion, thy God reigneth!" Isaiah 52:7

In accordance with the declaration pronounced by prophet Isaiah in the above verse,Sister Sarah Navaroji, Gods servant in the days of her youth has proclaimed the Salvation of Christ to the beloved Christian people of C.S.I Church , reminding them that 'Their Lord reigneth' , declaring the good tidings of good deeds and peace, toured around Marthandam,Vellalanvelai,Disayanvelai and many southern districts and spread the revival fire bringing Glory unto the name of the Lord and Blessings to Gods people.

It was in the year 1967 Sister preached in a CS I Convention at Vellalanvelai while in 1968 She addressed a CSI convention in Desayanvelai. Same year in 1968 Rev.Devasagayam and Rev.John invited Sister to Kanchirapuram in Marthandam for another CSI Convention.

. NEYVELI (1968)

Neyveli the small township with employees of N.L.C has been blessed with Sisters ministry. A revival meeting was arranged in Kalai Arangam Auditorium in Neyveli. The employees of the N.L.C Thermal Power Station have received fire power of the Holy Spirit through the anointed sermons of Sister Sarah Navaroji.New souls were also saved.

7. KARIYAVELAI, NEYYUR (1969)

Sister Navaroji visited Kariyavelai and Neyyur to preach Gods word in the CSI Convention meeting among the busiest schedule of other ministerial works in Madras(Chennai).

TIRUCHCHIRAPPALLI – (1969 – 2000)

Sister Navaroji made several crusade expeditions to Tiruchi fort armed with the sword of the Word of God. Procaliming the salvation Message of Jesus Christ she fought the spiritual battle to deliver those in the bondage of Satan the enemy.

In 1969 Sister addressed a Good News meeting invited by Dr.Maduram at Puthur in Tiruchi. Dr.Maduram was very sick when he arranged this Gospel meeting. As soon as Sister arrived Tiruchy she straight went to see Dr.Maduram and prayed for him.. He received complete healing by Sisters prayer and participated in the meetings with renewed strength.

In the years 1972 and 1973 she preached in the revival meetings arranged in Crawford ground, Tiruchi.Various denominational churches joined together to arrange such meetings. In 1983 Pastor. Easter Doss of a Penteostal Church invited Sister to speak in a good news meeting.In the year 2000, one beloved Sister namely Pushpam arranged revival meeting in YMCA through Pastor.Gnanadoss and invited Sister to preach .Due to this crusade visits Sister planted two new Pentecostal Churches in Tiruchi which in later days produced dedicated servants of God who have started ministries in various other places. The Lord touches some tribals

In this crusade on a particular day inspired by the Spirit of God Sister had shared her personal life testimony. At the end of the meeting a group of nomadic tribal people(Narikuravars) met Sister Navaroji and told her that they all wanted to know about Sister's personal life testimony and God granted their hearts desire that day. So, the whole crowd of tribal people gave their lives to Jesus and took immerse water Baptism and joined the Church.

9. MADURAI (Thirumangalam, Thamkkam Ground) – (1970 – 2000)

Sister Sarah Navaroji invaded Madurai the Tamil Literary center with the Gospel of Jesus Christ several times from the year 1970 to 2000. Madurai is the native of Sister Navaroji's parents,grand parents and great grand parents.Hence, she considered it a great privilege to minister in this soil .

In the Year 1970, February Sister was invited by CSI Church to speak in their Annual Convention. The same year in the month of December Sister was invited by a believer namely Jothi for a revival meeting organized by all Churches in Madurai.It was in November same year Sister visited Usillampatti near Madurai being invited by one brother namely Chellappa who was the Principal of Devar College.In the year 1972, August Sister preached in a revival meeting in Thirumangalam a small town near Madurai. Due to Sisters ministry a new Pentecostal church was planted in Thirumangalam. Pastor.Victor Seeni had been given the responsibility of this Church..In the year 1982 June all churches including C.S.I and Pentecostal churches organized a Perinba Peruviza Crusade in Thamukkam ground of Madurai. Sister delivered unadulterated Gospel in these meetings. She stressed the need of immerse water baptism for the born-again experience of every believer.

According to God's counsel inthe word of God many people who heard this message have taken immerse water Baptism. Those who opposed to this teaching also later on got convinced and obeyed for immerse water Baptism.So many have received the anointing of the Holy Spirit.

Later in the year 1987 Pastor.Masilamani of Indian Church of God and in the year 2000 Pastor.Jesudoss of Church of Jesus have invited Sister to speak in the revival meetings of their churches. All the meetings in Madurai were conducted in the famous Thamukkam ground. People gathered in large crowds. Madurai has experienced a great spiritual revival due to these repeated crusades. The Lord has granted a bountiful harvest.

HERE IS A TESTIMONY FROM MADURAI THE SOIL OF

SISTER NAVAROJI'S ANCESTORS

a) Dr.MIRIYAM BENEDICTA SURIYADEVI M.Sc., M..Phil., M.Ed., Ph.D.

(POST GRADUATE TEACHER ,Jeevana school, Madurai)

I was born in a highly traditional Lutheran and C.S.I. Christian background. Also as the only daughter to my parents, I was brought up in a good standard of life comforts with high level education. However, I lacked a personal encounter with Jesus, the Head of the Church and the Family.

My mother is the first cousin of the most saintly Servant of God

Sister Dr. Sarah Navaroji . In the year 1970, I met her in a

family gathering. The few moments I shared with her very closely

changed my entire life and it led me to have a personal encounter

with Jesus.

In the same year Sister Sarah Navaroji came to Madurai to preach in a crusade at Thamukkam Grounds. I attended the meeting all the days. After the meetings I obeyed God's word through Immerse Baptism in water and was born again. Before entering into the water Sister Navaroji laid her hands on me and prayed. Immediately I received the anointing of the Holy Spirit.

 I was led into deeper commitment. I forsook my outward apparels of gold and silver jewelry.

It is since then, till today the warmth continues.

I Praise God for it!

Dr.   Miriam   Benedicta

Suriyadevi

KOVILPATTI, THENKASI,SENGOTTAI , SIVAKASI,

VIRUDUNAGAR– (1970 , 1971)

" The harvest truly is plenteous, but the labourers are few; Pray ye therefore the Lord of the harvest, that he will send forth labourers into his harvest."Mathew 9:37,38

Thus asked Jesus his disciples. True to this statement many are still living in false belief and sin without knowing the true God and not heard the Gospel of salvation. Faithful believers who realized the imminent need to tell such people about the true God and preach the Gospel of salvation so that their souls may be harvested for the kingdom of God in Kovilpatti , Sengottai and Virudunagar area Pentecostal Churches have organized Crusades and invited Sister to come and minister to them. Sister Navaroji visited them on their invitation and preached in the revival meetings. God gave the harvest.Many in this places became true disciples of Jesus Christ.

OOTY, KODAIKKANAL, CUNOOR (Nilgiris) –(1970 -1980)

"Believe on the Lord Jesus Christ, and you shall be saved and your house."Acts 16:31

So says the Apostles Paul and Silas that men have to believe on Lord Jesus Christ to be saved from their sin. This Gospel of Jesus Christ is being preached all over the world and multitude of people are accepting Lord Jesus Christ into their lives and getting saved from their sin and curse.

The coldest places of Tamil Nadu also visited by Sister Sarah Navaroji to spread the revival fire. Missionary Union of India invited Sister to Kodaikkanal for preaching in some revival meetings in September 1970 and February 1973.Sister preached the fiery sermons of salvation to people who were enjoying a chill climate at Cunoor of Nilgiris in 1971 & 1972 and in 1980 at Ooty area.

COIMBATORE (1980,2000)

The Industrial works hub of Tamil Nadu had been ushered to work in the vineyard of Lord Jesus Christ. In the year 1980' Irai Vakku Illa Eyakkam ' a Gospel movement group have arranged for a Gospel meeting in the Chidambaram Stadium in which Sister Navaroji delivered the word of God. Again in the year 2000 Jesus Miracle Ministries organized a three days crusade in which Sister addressed the gathering with the Gospel of Christ.

4.6.5. Other Places in Tamil Nadu (1974 – 2002)

 From the year 1974 till 2002 Sister Sarah Navaroji had relentlessly made storming tours into many parts of Tamil Nadu and preached the Gospel of truth and gathered many many souls in the fold of the great Shepherd Lord Jesus Christ.

Here are some places listed without much briefing.

1. DINDUGAL – In 1974 believers in Dindugal arranged a Crusade and in the year 1980 Pastor. Simon Paul of Dindugal Church arranged for a Gospel Meeting .Sister Sarah Navaroji was invited to preach in these meetings.

2. SALEM – Sister visited Salem in 1975.After the revival meetings Sister planted a new Pentecostal Church and made one Sister.Jayamani in charge .

3. DONAVOOR -In 1979 Sister spoke in a C.S.I convention meeting.

4. THIRUVANNAMALAI, - In the year 2002, Pastor.Panneer Selvam of Magimayin Raja Church(King of Glory Church) invited Sister to Speak in their Revival Meeting.

HERE WE READ THE PERSONAL TESTIMONY OF PASTOR.PANNEER SELVAM

a) Rev.SAM.S.PANNEER SELVAM

It was by the grace and guidance of God I went to attend the Crusade at S.I.A.A. grounds Chennai. The divine melodious songs and anointed messages of Sister Sarah

Navaroji in the meetings inspired me and paved a way for the growth of my Spiritual Life.

Songs like   1. 'Aanandamai inbakkannan - yeagiduvanin
                              ;;   Thooyapithavin   mugam tharisippane '   Song No.41

                              (meaning)
                    'O,the   joyful   sweet   Cannan   –shall   I reach

            and behold the face of the Holy Father
                    'Valiba naalil yesuvai kandane'
                  (meaning)
          I found Jesus in the days of my youth

Have inspired me. I became a regular member in Z.G.P.F. Church. I was

in the Chruch for many years and was playing key board music.

 Sister also gave me an opportunity to compose and play music for one of her album namely

'Kaettal koduppaen'

Due to the prophetic anointed teachings of Sister Sarah Navaroji from the Bible ,I had grown in my spiritual life and today I am Pastoring a Church in Thiruvannamalai with 15 branch Churches. I am in the Lords service for the past 19 years. Praise God!

    Pastor.Sam .P.Panneerselvam

4.6.6. Southern Parts of Tamil Nadu (1978 – 2003)

Christian believers from southern part of Tamil Nadu were always enthusiastic to invite Sister Sarah Navaroji for

Crusades in various parts. Here are some places where Sister visited from 1978 to 2003 period.

a) NAGARKOIL   -   1978

b) KULASEGARAM -   2000

c) PAGODU   -   2002

d) MATHUR   -   1965 – 2003 –To preach in the annual Convention meetings

of Pastor. J.Lazer Church.

4.6.7 Other States in India – (1969 – 2000)

Though not briefed, only the places of visits in other States with the year are mentioned below.

1) VIJAYAWADA, THENALI & GUNTOOR (A.P)   - 1969

2)   BANGALORE   in   Gymkana   ground   - 1972

3)   BOMBAY   Various   Tamil   Churches   - 1974, 1985

4)   PARASALA,   THIRUVALLA   (KERALA)   - 1978

5)   CHIRLA   (A.   P   )   - 1979

6)   BHUVANESWAR   (ORISSA   )   - 1990

7) JAMMU, DELHI, BIHAR, CHANDIGAR, HOOBLI,

NAGPOOR - 1990 - 2000

Sister has translated some of her Tamil songs in Hindi, Telugu and Malayalam to sing
and teach in the respective languages while she ministered in other States.

In the Northern States Sister Sarah visited mainly the

Tamil populated places and Churches to encourage them with the word of God in Tamil while they lived far away from their native places and seldom listen the Bible in their mother tongue.

However, the native people also invited Sister to preach to them.

The Lord accompanied Sister Sarah Navaroji and the group of believers wherever they went and thr good Lord has performed great miracles.

HERE WE READ THE FIRST HAND INFORMATION TESTIMONY OF ONE OF OUR CHURCH ELDERS ACCOMPANIED SISTER IN THE NORTH INDIA CRUSADES.

a) Brother. Y.EDWARD , B.E

Superintendenting Engineer(Retd)

Tamil Nadu Slum Clearance Board

Sister Sarah Navaroji has toured all the states in India and also many foreign countries carrying the Gospel of Lord Jesus Christ. Sister herself has testified to us many miracles the Lord has performed during these crusades.

I wish to testify here a small incident which took place when I was in the group of believers with Sister in the North Indian Gospel tour.

In the year 1985, we have toured Haryana, Delhi and came to Nagpoor. There in Nagpoor a three days Gospel Meetings were arranged and Sister Navaroji preached the Word of God. After these three days meetings, on Saturday at 1.00 P.M we had to catch the train going to Chennai via Nagpoor from Delhi. We were to definitely board this train because the next day being Sunday Sister had to conduct the Sunday service back in our Chennai Church. Only few seats will be available in this train passing via Nagpoor to Chennai.We were four and many passengers were also waiting to go to Chennai.While we were prayerfully waiting at the Station the train arrived.

What has Happened was this:-

They started announcing in the broadcast the names of those for whom seats were allotted to go to Chennai. First Name was Sister Sarah Navaroji and then followed by other three of our names were called out and the broadcast stopped at that.

We knew no bounds of joy and praised our Lord for this miracle.

4.7   CRUSADES   AND   GOSPEL   MEETINGS ABROAD

" You will receive Power when the Holy Spirit comes on you; and you will be my

witnesses in Jerusalem, and in all Judea, and in all Samaria, and to the ends of the earth." Acts 1:8

According to this verse, Sister Sarah Navaroji filled with the Power of the Holy Spirit and commissioned by the Lord for His ministry has first witnessed in her own city Madras, then in her own state Tamil Nadu and in her own country India and then to all over the world in other countries.

Sister Sarah Navaroji with her other elder Sisters visited countries in U.S.A, Canada, Europe, Africa, Arabia and Asia.She Proclaimed the unadulterated Gospel of Jesus Christ and stressed the necessity of Holy Life in every believers life to please the Lord. She preached the Gospel to various color and race of people in Indian Culture which is more close to the holiness expected by the Lord than of any other nations culture.

Sister preached in house meetings, church meetings and public meetings gathered in various auditoriums.

4.7.1 United States Of America

1) AMERICA – (1985, 1987, 1989)

In the year 1985 Sister Navaroji with her other two elder Sisters visited Oklahama and New York in U.S.A and attended a world Christian Leaders Conference. During this time a number of Gospel meetings were arranged for Sister where she preached the word of God. All the Tamil Christian churches invited Sister to speak in their meetings several times.

Again in the year 1987 and 1989 Sister had been invited to U.S.A and totally five times she visited U.S.A and ministered to the churches. Dr.Samuel Johnson testifies that he has taken care of Sister Navaroji and other two Sisters during their visit to New York and he had the privilege of arranging their stay in his home.In U.S.A Sister toured to Los Angels and Dallas to minister to the Tamilians and Europeans there. Dr.Ranjit Singh a resident of U.S.A a firm believer of the Lord has also taken the responsibility of taking Sister Navaroji with other sisters to various meetings they were ministering.

A MIRACLE IN THE TOUR

a) Dr. Samuel Johnson

After concluding her ministry in New York ,Sister Sarah Navaroji and others came to John.F.Kennedy Air Port to go to Dallas. Since it was already time for the departure of the Plane, Dr.Samuel Johnson who accompanied them told Sister that they cannot travel now and they have to take the next flight. But Sister Navaroji said to him making a faith confession that the Lord will definitely make them fly in the same Aeroplane because they have the Scheduled meeting in Dallas.

What Happened? .... When the Sisters reached the Airport the door of the Aeroplane was already shut and about to move on the runway. But when an Airport manager sighted these Sisters, he said three Sisters dressed in white like angels have come to board the plane and immediately halted the Aircraft.Sister Sarah and other Sisters were given a V.I.P treatment and made to board the plane.

Dr.Samuel Johnson says it is a miracle and cannot happen otherwise.

2) CANADA – (1987)

In Canada Sister Navaroji ministered in Torando. Here all the Tamil Christians gathered bringing with them their friends of non- Christans also to hear the Gospel of Jesus Christ.

4.7.2. European Countries

1) U.K –(1985, 1987, 1989)

Bishop. Ramse invited Sister Sarah Navaroji to London for the world Christian Leaders Conference. Sisters missionary trip to London U.K was in total 7 times. Every time she visited U.S.A knowing her coming the churches in London use to invite her to visit them as well apart from the visits she made separately being invited by Pastor. Kumar of Ceylonese Tamil Church. Other English Churches also invited Sister.

2)   GERMANY, PARIS,SWITZERLAND,NETHERLANDS,
       AUSTRALIA (1987 - 1990)

The Ceylonese Tamil Christian believers who resettled in these European countries have invited

Sister Sarah Navaroji to minister to them in their Churches. In 1987,Sister made her missionary visit to

Frankfurt and Essen in Germany and then to Netherlands. Pastor. Francis of a Ceylonese Tamil Christian Church invited Sister Navaroji to Australia where she preached in their church in Brisbane. The other English churches also invited her to minister to them. She also addressed in a Spanish church there. Sister gave special message to the Australian Broadcasting Corporation also.

3) ARAB COUNTRIES – (1989)

Upon the invitations extended to Sister from the Tamil churches in Middle East

(Arab countries) Sister ministered in Muscat of Oman. Gospel Meetings here were arranged by Pastor. David Gurudoss. Sister Navaroji visited Sharjah of U.A.E in February 1989, Dubai and Abu Dhabi of U.A.E in March 1989. Pastor.J.Edwin Rajkumar of Dubai Tamil Church arranged for a series of special revival meetings there.The Tamil believers learnt lot of Sisters' songs and bought lot of Song Cassettes so that they can keep hearing the songs.

4) AFRICAN COUNTRIES – (1990)

Sister Sarah Navaroji with her two other elder Sisters under took missionary tour

to Ethiopia and Zimbabwe upon special invitations.Muthananda Swamigal invited

Sister to Harare in Zimbabwe to address in special meetings for Tamils and to

other country believers. Later she visited Adisababa. Sister ministered to them in

Indian culture stressing the high morale code expected from believers holy life.

5) ASIAN COUNTRIES- (1982 – 1992)

The Asian countries Sister received invitation to Minister are PHILIPINES in 1988.

To SINGAPORE Sister visited upon an invitation from Assemblies of God.Enroute
the three Sisters visited MALAYSIA in the year 1982.Again in the years 1988 and
1992 they visited Singapore and Malaysia. Sister preached in Tamil Churches, house
meetings and other nationality people also been ministered in these countries.

6) JERUSALEM

Sister's Jerusalem visit is of great importance. She was overwhelmed to see the places with her own eyes where the Lord was born, ministered, crucified and rose again about which she composed many songs visualizing the places in her spirit. When she came to the garden of Gethsemane pondering over the agony and sufferings of our Master a heart melting song emanated from the depth of her heart and instantly she composed and sung it there.

" Endan Yesuvudan
Intha Getsemaneyil
En aathuma kadhariyae
Aandavarai noaki mandraaduthey"   Song No.247
(meaning)
" With my Jesus
in this Gethsemane
my soul crieth - and
intercedes to the Lord.

On Mount Olives Sister addressed in a Church of God Congregation also.

4.8 Prophetical Ministry

The Prophetical ministry of Sister Sarah Navaroji has been an integral part of all the other ministries. To meet the various spiritual and physcical need of people such as healing, guidance, counseling or warning she spoke the utterances as given by the Holy Spirit during her sermon, public prayer from pulpit or during personal prayer to individuals. Such prophetical words from Sister Navaroji had been as promises of God or revelations in order to edify, exhort and admonish people who came to her to be ministered.

WE WOULD LIKE TO PRESENT FEW EXAMPLES HERE WHICH WILL JUST BE A DROP OF WATER FROM THE OCEAN (OR) AN HANDFUL OF SAND FROM THE SEA SHORE.

a) Brother. M.D. EDWIN ,T.N. Agricultural Department,

(Retd   ),

Chennai

I hail from a good Christian Family . In the year 1974 my elder Sister suddenly passed away. Unable to bear the sorrow my mother attempted to commit suicide by consuming sleeping pills.

It was at that time my father found a hand bill about the Gospel Crusade Sister Sarah Navaroji was conducting at S.I.A.A grounds Chennai.

He took all of us for that Crusade.

During the preaching time Sister Navaroji prophetically called out saying 'One Sister is here thinking of committing suicide . By doing so, you cannot see your daughter, but you will go to hell. Change your mind.'

Immediately my mother surrendered her life to Jesus. Then we all went to ZION GOSPEL PRAYER FELLOWISHIP CHURCH and became members. Then on my mother started living a blessed life filled with peace and happiness from the Lord.

God gave me a permanent Government job also and has been doing many miracles for our family.

Praise God.

M.D.Edwin

b)   Sister   ESTHER   RANI, Chennai.

(A testimony given by Brother.Victor Elango about his mother Esther Rani.)

My mother Esther Rani was tormented by evil spirits attack terribly from the early days of her married life. As a Christian family we were

ashamed of an evil spirit possession on one of our family members.

We took our mother to many Christian meetings and got prayed for her

 by the servants of God.

Esther Ra

After suffering for 20 years, some members of the Zion GospelPrayer Fellowship Church invited us to come to their worship service.

 Sister Sarah Navaroji prayed for my mother and prophetically told us to

regularly come for Sunday Worship Service and that the evil spirit will go away.

 As we continued the same way the evil spirit left our mother without any prior information.

Also when my mother was diagnosed for cancer at the age

of 40 , Sister Navaroji prayed and God healed her.   At the age of 67, my mother happily passed away to be with the Lord. She was very active serving the Lord all along her life.   Praise the Lord !

Victor Elango

c) Evangelist.Dr.CLIFFORD KUMAR

I was born in a Christian family but we did not know Christ the way it should be.Our family enemies have done witchcraft against us due to which I suffered heavy financial losses. Furthermore, I was diagnosed for cancer disease. Many Gods people prayed for me. Some of my friends have performed their own religious rites also for my deliverance.

In the year 1972, one of my Hindu friend took me to the S.I.A.A. grounds, Chennai Crusade. In the meeting Sister Sarah Navaroji prophetically said in her preaching from Bible verse Numbers 23 : 23

"There is no enchantment against Jacob, neither is there any divination against Israel".   Don't you Know this? Twice she said this for me, I believed.Hearing this prophetic word my Hindu friend told me "Your God will not forsake you".

After coming back home, I fully surrendered my life to Jesus Christ. Jesus delivered me from all the witchcraft bondages. I dedicated myself for doing the Lords Service full time.   Now I am 80 years old still I am running for the service of my Lord Jesus.
Praise God!.

Evnag. Dr. Clifford Kumar

d) Evangelist. NELLAI JEBARAJ.

Brother Nellai Jebaraj was an Evangelist powerfully used by Lord Jesus Christ. Many are those who were saved and countless are those who have been delivered from the bondage of evil spirits. Through his gifted ministry there are many testimonies who have been released from the clutches of witchcrafts.

When Sister Sarah Navaroji was preaching in a crusade at Palayamkottai, she spoke a prophetic word from the Lord towards Brother Nellai Jebaraj who was sitting behind the steering wheel of his car. She said,

'Young man, God is calling you for the ministry . Don't delay !.

Brother Nellai Jebaraj who at first hesitated but later obeyed the call of God given to him through the prophetic word of Sister Sarah Navaroji . He was a channel of blessing to millions through his ministry filled with many spiritual gifts from the Lord.

Glory to God!.

e)Rev.Dr.V.ALBERTJAYASINGH   -   University of Jerusalem, Chennai

I have been an admirer of Sister Sarah Navaroji and her Ministries from my youth. I fondly listen to her songs and messages which have inspired me a lot.

In the year 2010 November, I went to meet Sister Navaroji along with my son Ebenezer to pray for us. She prayed for us and prophetically told ' you will do the ministry of Planting Churches'. I could not believe because, I founded a Bible College but did not like to do Church ministries.

The very next week I had to go to Odhissa on my missionary work. There I had to take up the responsibility of 333 Churches at once. Sister Sarah Navaroji's prophetic word fulfilled there.

Now in Tirunelveli District in 10 villages we have established Churches in the name of 'Church of Jerusalem'.

By the end of 2012 we have planned to plant more than 100 Churches in India and Abroad.

I thank God and also appreciate Rev. Dr. R. Samuel for writing this book 'Lily Among Thorns'., who has done his Ph. D. Degree in our university. I praise God for all the blessings I received through Sister.Sarah Navaroji's ministries.

Praise be to God !.

Rev. Dr. V. Albert Jayasingh

CHAPTER 5 - Song Ministry

Song Ministry

5.1 Introduction

The Song Ministry of Sister Sarah Navaroji is popular and well known all over the world especially among the Tamil Christian population. Her songs are sung in Tamil Churches of all denominations like R.C, C.S.I, C.P.M, Pentecostal, Full Gospel etc. She started composing and singing songs at the age of around sixteen itself. While she was in High School final she composed and sung a song for interschools competetion on the theme UNO which has won the first prize. That was her first experience of composing song. After Sister Sarah Navaroji was born again, the divine gift of composing soul inspiring songs descended on her. So, In the year 1956 she composed a song that invites sinners to Jesus Christ for eternal life. It goes like this:-

" Yesuvandai Vaarayo nee
Nithiya Jeevan Vendikolvai
Maiyaana Inbam Thandhu
    Nithiya Motsham serpaar meiyaai"   Song No.65- Christian Songs of Joy

Song Book

(meaning)

'' Would you come to Jesus and
Intercede for eternal life
With the true joy He will
Reach you to heaven for sure.

In the year1959, while in prayer only with her elder Sister in the CPM Church Sister Navaroji was filled with the Holy Spirit. She heard a sweet melodious song sung by a group of angels. She captured the wordings and the tune of that song and as soon as returning home, Sister Sarah wrote down and composed this wonderful song giving appropriate tune in line with the tune sung by the angels which is in the top list of her Hit songs till today.

Here is that most wonderful song(in Tamil):-

"Unnadamaanavarin Uyarmaraivilirukkiravan
　　　　Sarva vallavarin Nizhalil thanguvaan"
Song No.120- CSJ Song Book
The song is the true extract of Psalm 91

(meaning)

" He who dwells in the shelter of the
most High
will rest in the shadow of the Almighty
This is a great privilege."

When she entered the full time ministry and joined the C.P.M Church in the year 1960 in Ceylon, the church Pastors there recognized her gift of composing songs and gave the responsibility of composing Tamil songs for congregational singing and teach the same to others in the church. She composed many wonderful songs like :-

'Aanandamai Naame Aarbarippome ' Song No.;.7 – 'Let us make Joyful noise'

'Thothirum paadiye potriduven'   Song No;.4 - 'I will sing praise and give thanks'

'Thooya thooya devanai naam -potri' Song.No;.6 - 'We will praise the Holy, Holy God'

It was during one of those days she composed the song,

" Thudithu paadida paathirame
        Thungavan yesuvin naamamide" Song No.5- Christian Songs of Joy Song Book

(meaning)
"Worthy to be praised
Wonderful Name of Jesus"

But the chief Pastor Alwin did not approve this song. He gave the reason saying that the tune was

so marvelous that people who listen and sing this song will give glory to the composer instead of God. However, it was accepted at a later stage and is being sung in C.P.M church and everywhere till to-day.

Later, when she came to Madras from Ceylon in the year 1962 and had to start her own ministry, Sister utilized her gift of songs to the full extent for the glory of God.

Jesus said in Mathew 5: 15,

" Neither do people light a lamp and put it under a bowl. Instead, they put it on its stand,

and it gives light to everyone in the house."

Similarly, Sister Navaroji lighted the gift of Christian songs creativity and put it on the appropriate pedestal only to glorify God.

Further Jesus added in Mathew 5: 15,

" In the same way, let your light shine before men, that they may see

your good deeds and praise your Father in heaven."

Even so did Sister Navaroji in letting the gift of a divine poetess within her to shine before the people of all nations so that those who listened to her songs all over the world praised the heavenly father for the blessings they received through them.Sister Sarah Navaroji's songs are unique in that the songs are composed, tuned and sung by herself unlike others in which the songs are composed by a composer and tuned by some one else and sung by another talented singer. The tunes are of her own and not copied from others songs.Also,they are of standard and approved melodies and not any haphazard tunes just for singing.

The inspiration to compose songs descends on her in various ways.

1)When she passes certain situations,the still voice of the Lord speaking to her through   that situation will induce a song within.

2)The songs flow out from the depth of her heart very relevant to the particular occasion in which she is ministering.

3)While meditating the Scripture, a particular verse in a chapter or the whole chapter in the Scripture will emerge as a song.

4)Many a times while in prayer or meditation she use to hear angels singing certain

Song which Sister would capture in her mind and not verymuch later would compose

The song with appropriate melodious tunes.

5) Even while in deep sleep she use to get the tunes in dream which she was able to

retrieve and compose soul stirring songs.

6) Sister Sarah Navaroji has composed Songs suitable to be sung during Church worship

services, special Church services and meetings with various to headings incorporating

Bible verses extensively.

*To give us a clear insight few examples of Songs composed with above said kind of inspirations are illustrated in the following few pages.

*Further more, Songs under different headings are also enumerated with appropriate Bible references.

5.2 The background for Songs Creation – Few examples

In the year 1960, when Sister Sarah Navaroji was chosen for the ministry in CPM Church, she was posted to Ceylon. To go to Ceylon she has to take a Ship voyage from Dhanushkodi for which she has to go from Chennai Egmore by train. She boarded the train at Egmore and as she was waiting for her mother to come to see her off , mother didn't come for a long time. Thinking that mother may not come, her heart sunk in deep sorrow. Consoling herself that even if mother forgets the Lord will not forget her, she composed the following song, in 1960.

(Transliteration of Tamil Song)
"Ennai maravaa Yesu naada
Unthan dayavaal ennai nadathum

Thaai than sayaai maranduvittalum

Unnai maraven endradale

thothirum" Song No. 39- Song Book

(meaning)

" O,Jesus who never forget me

Lead me on by your mercy

Mother may forget her child - but

I will never forget ,you said- Praise you

Lord!"

Actually her mother was waiting in another platform of Egmore Station by mistake. She arrived at the last minute to the right platform and sent her off waving her hands. Countess people have received consolation from their grief by singing this song down through the years.

2. In the year 1962,in Ceylon, some disturbing situations arouse in the CPM Church. It was a question mark whether she can continue her ministry there. While diligently seeking the Lord's guidance for the next step, Sister Navaroji surrendered to God's will and prayed. She composed her prayer as a song which till today is of immense help to all those who seek God's guidance. Here is that song presented in Transliterated Tamil and meaning in English:

En karam pidithenrum nadathidumae

En sitham ennil ondrum niraivera

virumbenae

Um sitham pola ennai nadathidum

paramesa" Song No.38 –Song Book

(meaning)

" I surrender all to you Jesus

Hold my hand and lead me
I shall never like my will
Lead me as you will – dear Lord!

At this troubled time Sister Sarah Navaroji's mother and elder Sister went to Ceylon and brought her back to Madras (Chennai), India.

3.In the year 1962, after returning to Madras and had just started her own ministry,

wondering the miraculous way the Lord is leading her even as He lead the ancient saints, she composed a poem with a heartful of gratitude to the Lord which means :-

" Work of the Lord is awesome and wonderful
With the ancient saints –and
God whom our forefathers trusted – is
Unchanging yesterday to-day and for ever."
(Transliteration of Tamil Song)

" Aacharyamae athisayame
Aandavar seyalgal Aathi baktharidam
Nam murpidakkal nambina thevan
Netrum indrum endrum maaridarae"
Song No.125

4.In 1967, for the Good Friday service Sister Sarah composed a special song with the following meaning

" He lay his head , hung on the cross afflicted,
Pronouncing last seven words, the Lord died there
Cried Jesus saying Father forgive them
For they know not what they do."
(Transliteration of Tamil Song)
"Siluvai meedil thalayai saaithu
Sirumaiyutravar thonginaar

Kadaisi eazhu vaakku uraithu
Karthar angae marithaar
Mannithidum, Pithavae neer
Enna saiginromendru
Indru evargal arinthidaargal yendresu katharinaar."   Song No.157

5.1n 1975, while Pastor Lazarus was giving message in her church about the preparedness of believers for the second coming of Lord Jesus Christ Sister instantly composed the following song on the same subject which later drawn many lukewarm and backslidden believers to the Lord.

" I am prepared to meet the Lord
I shall have eternal joy
In the mid air
King Jesus I'll see."
(Transliteration of Tamil Song)
" Naan Aayathamaanaen Aandavarai santhikka
Nithiya magizhchi adaivain
Madhiya aagaya meethilae
Mannan Yesuvai Kaanuvain.   Song No.193- in Christian Songs of Joy

Song Book

6. In 1980, when her nephew (elder sister's son)Johnny got married she composed a wonderful wedding song,
" Bless us Lord
With thy Loving hands
O' Our eternal God Jesus
Shine thy face so great"
The later stanzas of this song are the true extracts of Psalm

128, the song of a blessed family.
(Transliteration of Tamil Song)
" Aaseervadhitharulum Deva
Anbu niraintha karangalal
Engal Aadhi Devan Yesuvae
Thiru mugathai pragaasiyum.   Song No.225- in CSJ Song Book

7. In the year 1984 when Sister's mother Soundaram Asirvatham died , She composed a song calling her mother a pearl inside the shell, and acknowledging all the troubles her mother went through in the last days are for good as said in Psalm 119: 71
" It was good I'm afflicted
I learnt thy righteous statues
I received eternal glory
Like a pearl within a shell
Those who are dead in the Lord
At the blow of trumpet - should fly away.
(Transliteration of Tamil Song)
" Naan ubathiravappattathu nallathu
Needhi pramanathai katrukkondane
Nithiya magimaiai petrukkondane,
Chippikkul nal muthu pole
Kartharukkul marithore
Ekkalam thonikayil yegi parandhidavae.
Song No.235 -in CSJ Song Book

5.3 Songs Compiled – The Song Book
Sister Sarah Navaroji has so far composed about 400 Tamil

Christian Songs apart from English songs and choruses. All these songs are compiled in a Song book published by Sister called

" CHRISTIAN SONGS OF JOY." And in Tamil this song book is named as

" Kiristhava Aananda Keedangal"

They are Registered by the ' Registrar of Copy Rights, Govt. of India.'

The Song Nos. mentioned against each song in the above narrative is the number of that particular song in this Song book of latest edition.

All these songs are available now in MP3 CDs, Video DVDs and Pendrive.

Recording of these songs were done in reputed studios in Madras (Chennai).

Initially the responsibility of recording, production and distribution was given to HMV company. They had Sister Sarah Navaroji as their artist. The songs were recorded in Gramophone record plates. The HMV company has done a remarkable job in recording,producing and distributing the songs. Sister's songs were relayed continuously from All India Radio- Chennai Radio Station in the 'Bakthi Paadalgal'(Devotional Songs) program. Sister had requested some renowned singers like Seergazhi Govindarajan, Vani Jayaram to sing some of her songs also.

At a later stage Sister Sarah Navaroji has taken the total responsibility of singing, recording, producing and distributing by herself. The Songs were recorded in Cassette tapes once the Gramophone record plates became obsolete. Keeping at pace with advancing technology, the songs got recorded in CDs and then in MP3 CDs and now have come out in Video DVDs.

The well known *Music Directors namely Sathyvictor, Kalyanam, Mangalamoorthy, Henry Daniel, Richard Vijay, Andrew and Augustine have provided the back ground music for Sisters songs at different times for different albums.

Sister Sarah Navaroji6
with Co Singers in
Recording Studio

*Pastor. Vincent Samuel, Brother.Victor Philip,Pastor Finny Joseph, Pastor Alex Joseph and Pastor Rabindran have also played back ground music to many Sister Sarah Navaroji's popular songs during the days of their early ministry when they were youths.

They all cherish the memory of those days.

Sister Sarah Navaroji with Music Director7
and Sound Engineer at Recording Studio

HERE IS THEIR WITNESSES
a) Pastor. M.VINCENT SAMUEL
Sister Sarah Navaroji's mother Soundaram Asirvatham was
a Child Evangelist. During the year 1960 when I was a
young boy, I attended a Sunday Class session where she
was teaching the Gospel of Jesus Christ to children in the
Tamil Baptist Church, Kilpauk.
It was there I gave my life to Jesus. After my schooling, I
joined Bible College and then entered the Lord's ministry
full time.

Rev.Dr. M.Vincent Samuel

During my youth days, I was very much inspired by the
songs of

Sister Sarah Navaroji and I had the opportunity to play
some music

for her songs recordings. Eventually, the soul stirring
songs of Sister Sarah Navaroji arouse the talent within me
to compose songs for the Lord.
By the grace of God I composed some famous songs like,

'Paralogame en sonthamae'   'Oh, the heaven,its my own'

'Vilainda palanai arupparillai'   'Alas, there is none to reap the ripe'

'Magimai matchimai niraindavarae' .   'O, thou full of glory and majesty'

For MPA.Church, Rohith Recordings, HMV, Interico and other Christian mission organizations.

Praise God !

Pastor. M.Vincent Samuel

b) Pastor. CHARLES FINNY JOSEPH.

MARANATHA   MINISTRIES, Chennai.

Beloved in the Lord, Greetings!

From the years of 1960s Sister Sarah Navaroji the zealous and committed servant of God has caused a great revival within the Christian Churches and outside as well through her Song Ministries and Crusades.

Pastor.Charles Finney   Joseph

In my personal life., I Praise God for those days in which

 I played some musical instruments to record her songs both in her Church and home along with Brother Sathi Victor,

 Victor Philip, (my brother- in-law.) ,Pastor Vincent Samuel and Pastor Rabinder.

Sisters songs are integrated with Bible Verses and I been edified by them. They have created a thirst within me for deeper commitment and enabled me to stand as an exemplary servant of God today.

Glory to God!

Pastor.Charles Finny Joseph.

5.4. Division of Songs

Sister Sarah Navaroji has composed, tuned and sung about 400 Tamil Christian songs in total and of varieties which are suitable for every occasion and festival. Songs are grouped under different headings . Some examples under each heading are briefed herewith.

The songs are presented in Transliterated Tamil and the meaning of them are hi-lighted in English for the reader to understand.

1) PRAISE & WORSHIP SONGS

Praise Songs

As we open the song book 'Christian Songs of joy' of Sister's Songs, we find that first few songs(Song No.2 to Song No.24) are Praise Songs. Then we find Praise songs in numbers 200, 281, 319, 320, 358 to 360.

It is because we have to Praise our Lord God first as we approach him. We are taught in the Scripture that our Lord dwells in Praises. The Holy angles continuously praise him. Prophet Isaiah says in Isaiah 6: 3 that Seraphs Praise the Lord saying

'Holy, Holy, Holy is the Lord Almighty'

Also we read in Revelation 4: 11 that the twenty four Elders and four living creatures Praise our God in heaven saying

" You are worthy, Our Lord God, to receive glory and honor and Power..."

The Psalmist says in Psalm 18: 3 ' I Call to the Lord, who is worthy of Praise.'

Further the Psalmist says in Psalm 150: 6

'Let every thing that has breadth Praise the Lord.'
Prophet Isaiah also confirms it in Isaiah 38: 18, 19 saying
' For the grave cannot Praise you.........

The living, the living ---- they
Praise you .'
Apostle Paul says
'Through Jesus , therefore, let us continuously offer to God a Sacrifice of Praise' Hebrews 13:15
One of the beautiful creations in the songs Sister Navaroji under this heading having the theme taken from Psalm 19: 1 to 4 verses and also from Psalm 148: 1 to 5 verses is found as
Song No. 3 in the 'Christian Songs of Joy ' Song book.
Song No. 3 Christian Songs of Joy
Chorus

Kadhiravan Thondrum kaalaiyidae

Pudhiya   kirubai
pozhindiduthe – nal

Thuthi   seluthiduvom
Yesuvukkae

Stanzas

1. Vaana sudargal kaanaga jeevan

Vaazhthidavae   Paran
matchimaiyae

Kaatru paravai ootru neerodai

Kartharukae   kavi
paadiduthae   - Kathiravan

6. Vaanam Boomi yavum padaitheer

Vaanam thirandae thondriduveer

Aaval adanga ennaiyum azhaikka

Aathuma   nesarae

vanthiduveer   - Kathiravan

Hi-lights of the song

Early in the morning as the sun rises the new grace of God is poured forth and

therefore let us offer the Sacrifice of Praises to Jesus our Lord even as all the creations

like Sun , Moon, Hill, Sea, , Animals and Birds Praise Him according to Psalm 148.

The song ends with the expression of the desire of a saint saying

          ' O' the beloved of my soul come soon.'

.

Worship Songs

Whenever the believers gather to-gather for Prayer meeting or Sunday Service or any other occasion the congregation worships the Lord with singing songs of exaltation and adoration.

The Psalmist says in Psalm 34: 3 ' Glorify the Lord with me;

          Let us exalt His name together.

The act of worshipping the Lord with glorifying and exalting His Name brings us close to the throne of His grace and we are wrapped up in His presence.

Further the Psalmist says in Psalm 95:6 'Come, let us bow down in worship,

          Let us kneel before the Lord our Maker;

Jesus answered Satan in Luke 4:8 quoting the scripture and`said,

" It is written: Worship the Lord your God and serve him only.'

The worship songs in the Song book is found mostly from Song No. 123 to 147, 267, 271 to 273, 278, 280, 283 to 287, 307, 332, 333, 336 & 372.

When the congregation gathers together, it is important to prepare ones mind and heart keeping away from all distractions and focus on the Lord alone to receive the word of God while effectively communicating with God to submit our intercessions, praises and thanksgiving. The worship songs do a great deal of such preparation of a believer in the sanctuary of God.

The following song is one of the hit songs of Sister Sarah Navaroji and is delightfully sung by Christian believers.

Song No. 280 in 'Christian Songs of Joy ' Song Book

Song No. 280 – Christian Songs of Joy

Chorus

    Sagala Deva Janangalae

                  Kaikotti Kartharai

     Gembeeramai paaduvom

Sub Chorus

Avar ratchippai suvisheshamaaga

               Agila   ulagamengum saatriduvom   Psalm 96: 2

  Stanza

      1. Parisuththa sthalamadilae

              Bayabakkthiyulla   janamai naam

              Yesudevanai   paadi thudhipom

              Idu   inbamum   ettradum nalladumae   - Sagala

Hi-lights of the song

The Song calls upon all God's people to clap their hands and sing with a great shout.

Also the song exhorts His people as Psalmist says in Psalm 96: 2

' Proclaim his Salvation day after day,

Declare his glory among the

nations.'

2) PRAYER SONGS

There are some songs that Sister Navaroji has grouped under 'Prayer Songs '.

These songs are found in the Song Book from Numbers 38 to 53, 247, 248, 265, 330, 367 & 368.   Some examples are given below which are self explanatory.

Before the congregation goes for Prayer or an individual goes to the presence of God for prayer these songs will encourage, exhort and increase the faith of the believers.

On of the popular song of Prayer taken here for example is Song Number.48 from the

'Christian Songs of Joy' Song book. Again it is self explanatory.

Song No;. 48 – Christian Songs of Joy

Chorus

Jebavalai emakkanandam – endrum

Jebamilla jeyamillai

Jebam engal jeyamae

Stanzas

1. Irul soozhntha vanam pondra irunda getsemaneyil

Irudivalayil jebitheer

Rattha vervayum perumootchum

perugidavo   - antha

                         Iravellam jebitheeraiaa
- inthe jebavalai Luke 22: 44

            8. Ninaiyadha nerathil thirudan pol varugindren
                         Nitham neengal vilithirungal
                         Endru phodanai alytheere adhai
nambiyae vandom

                         Emmakkunthan   belan
thaarumae   - inthe jebavalai

      Mathew 24:   42,43,44
Hi-Lights of the song
Here the praying believer quotes the references of effective
prayers that were answered and prays to God that His
prayer also be answered in the same manner.
He quotes the prayer of Jesus in Gatsemane. Song ends
with the exhortation that we should watch and pray
because the Lord will come in an unexpected hour.
3) ALTAR CALL SONGS
The Christian Crusades and Gospel meetings are held with
the purpose of winning souls for Christ. Hence, after
preaching the Good News of Salvation through Jesus
Christ in such meetings, an Altar Call is given open to all.
Those who are convicted and convinced of the Gospel will
come forward to surrender their lives to Jesus.
The songs that could be sung during such altar calls are
from the Song number.62 to 86,207,220, 258,261, 268,
306, 314,322 & 335 in the "Christian Songs of Joy" Song
book. These songs even when they were heard or sung at
home or else where, there are testimonies that people have

repented and submitted their lives to Jesus.

A popularly used Altar Call song is considered here. This song is used usually by Christian believers when they go for outreach to village ministries or street preaching. This song is also used in crusades and Gospel meetings during the altar call time.

The Song No. is 68 in the 'Christian Song of Joy ' Song book.

Song No. 68 – Christian Songs of Joy

Chorus

Varuvaai tharunamidhuvae alzhaikiraarae

Valla Aandavar Yesuvandai

Stanzas

4. Vaanathin   keezhae   boomi   melae
Acts 4 : 12

Vaanavar   Yesu naamamallal

Ratchippadaiya vazhi ellaiyae

Ratchagar   Yesu   vazhi avare   - Varuvaai

6. Saththiya Vaakkai Numbiyae vaa

Nithiya jeevan unakkalippaar

Un perai jeeva pusthagathil

Unmaiyai   indru ezhuthiduvaar   - Varuvai

Hi-Lights of the Song

A general call is given open to all to come to the mighty Lord Jesus giving an emphasis from

the verse Acts 4: 12 'Salvation is found in no one else, for there is no other name under heaven given to men by which we must be saved.' So, the last stanza invites to come believing the true word of God and Jesus will give eternal life and enter your name surely in the 'book of Life' to-day.

4) CHRISTMAS SONGS

Sister Sarah Navaroji has composed some special songs for using in the Christian festival seasons. Christmas is celebrated all over the world by Christians and non-Christians as well with much joy and enthusiasm. It is a month long celebration in Christian churches with carol singings and special song services. All over the world in all most all Tamil Christian churches many of the Christmas songs composed by Sister Navaroji is used in Night carol rounds and carol services. However, these songs can be sung at any time of the year to remember the birth of Jesus the Son of God. The Birth of Lord Jesus Christ is foretold or prophesied by the Prophets of Old Testament in the Holy Bible.

In Sister Sarah Navaroji's Songs on the birth of Jesus, she has meticulously quoted the Prophets' sayings and confirms that Jesus was born in the fulfillment of those prophesies.

The Christmas Songs or the Songs on the Birth of Jesus Christ is found in the following number of songs in the 'Christian Songs of Joy' song book.

Song numbers:- 1, 25, 87 to 104, 202, 211 to 217, 234, 240,241, 243 to 245, 284 to 294, 309, 326 to 328, 344, 363 and 365.

The purpose of these songs are not festival celebration or merry making. But the in-depth meaning of the songs proclaim the purpose and nature of the Birth of Jesus.The songs are the creation of a professional artist who is able to take those who sing these songs to the very place of the birth of Jesus. Not only that but also the eternal plan of the Almighty God the Father in sending His only begotten son to this world is vividly shown. The Birth of a great King who chose an humble manger as a very ordinary human being but greeted by both wise men and poor shepherds heralded by the heavenly host of angels are perfectly presented in soul thrilling poetic form.

A very popular Christmas Song is considered here which is sung in all the Tamil Churches during Christmas seasons. The number of this song is No.93 in the 'Christian Songs of Joy ' song book.

Song No.93 - Christian Songs of Joy
Chorus

> Pirandaar Pirandaar
> Vaanavar   puvi

maanidar pugazh

> Paadida Pirandaar

> Stanzas
> 1.   Maattu   thozhuvam

therindeduthar   Luke 2:7

> Maa Deva Devanae
> Maenmai veruthar thazhmai tharithaar
> Maa thyagiyai valarndhaar   -

Pirandaar

> 3. Yesu pirandaar ullamadhil

> Idhai engum saatriduvom
> Pusippum kudippum deva

rajjiyamalla   Romans 14: 17

Paran aaviyil

magizhvom   - Pirandaar

Hi-Lights of the song

He was born even as the earthly mankind and heavenly host sang praises. The great God has chosen a cattle shed, forsook exaltation and humbled himself.

The song challenges us to declare every where that Jesus is born in our hearts and that eating and drinking in festival celebration is not the Kingdom of God, referring to Romans 14: 17.

5) GOOD FRIDAY SONGS

Good Friday Songs are found in numbers 27,29,148 to 161,203,221,295 to 303 & 338.

Sister Sarah Navaroji has produced many moving and inspiring songs by surveying the wondrous cross that is performing the miraculous transformation in the lives of human beings. She brings out the reason so vividly as to why the Cross, which symbolizes a horrific form of capital punishment that was employed by the Roman Kings to suppress any rebellion against them, has become the sign of victory to Christians. She has based her reasons from the Holy Bible. The Bible teaches that forgiveness of sins and healing of sickness which constitutes the Salvation is made available to every one who believes, by the lashes Jesus received by the whipping of the ruthless Roman soldiers and the death of Jesus on the rugged cross. A prophet namely Isaiah who lived among Israelites during the period (792 B.C --- 722 B.C) has wrote in Isaiah 53:4,5 : " Surely he took up our infirmities

(Sickness) and carried our sorrows, ... He was pierced for our transgressions , he was crushed for our iniquities(Sins); the punishment that brought us peace

(Salvation) was upon him, and by his wounds we are healed (Physical and Spiritual).

 Sister has depicted in her songs the very scene of Jesus being nailed on the cross in his hands and legs, a crown of thorns pressed on his head. The precious blood of Jesus Christ without blemish which has gushed out from his wounds is the high price paid for redeeming man kind from the clutches of Satan who imprisoned them by the power of his darkness.(Reference: I Peter 1:18 & 19). That is how the Cross, a gruesome instrument of death, has become a 'holy glamour' and the only 'boast' of a Christian believer.

These so called Good Friday songs are sung during the Holy Communion services and also in the Gospel meetings which has become a source of many souls being saved and added to the Church of Jesus Christ all over the world.

Here we consider one such song composed by Sister Navaroji. The song takes us to the very spot where Jesus was crucified.

The song number is No.158 in the 'Christian Songs of Joy' song book.

Song No 158 – Christian songs of Joy

Chorus

Antho calvary maettinil

Anbulla Yesu raja

Thongum seluvai katchiyae

Thangum en sinthayilae

Stanzas

2. kadiyallo thgathirko   John 19:29

Karthavae petrukkondeer

Endan paavathin kasappiyum

        Yesuvae   rusithu
maandirae   - Antho

    5. Ratchanyamae siluvayin

        Raththathal
kandadainthane   Hebrews 9: 28
        Nandri pongida nokiduvain
        Numbikkai   eantha   en
Yesuvae   - Antho

Hi- Lights of the Song

The Song starts saying that the horrific sight of the loving King Jesus hanging on the cross shall stay in my mind. The second stanza refers the verse John 19:29
that a bitter vinegar was given to him for his 'thirst' to symbolize his tasting of our sins bitterness. The last stanza clearly states that the Salvation is from the blood shed on the cross and thereby we are given a hope for which we praise God with our heartful of gratitude. Hebrews 9: 28 explains about this hope.

6) EASTER SONGS

Sister Sarah Navaroji has composed several songs under the title 'Easter Songs' which describe in detail about the resurrection of Jesus on the third day after his crucifixion.

Sister Navaroji has inserted a lot more scripture verses than her own wordings in the Easter Songs as her usual methodology to illustrate the events related to the resurrection of Jesus on the third day and witnessed by the women and disciples at the open tomb. The death is vanquished and the grave is conquered when Jesus came alive out of the tomb on the third day.

Resurrection of Jesus Christ is the central theme of Christianity without which it would have been a dead religion. This Radiant and still Radiating historical fact around which the Christian Theology revolves around is the one and the only reason that has weathered out all the arguments and claims against the Truth related to Jesus Christ the Son of God for the past 2000 years.

Sister links in these songs the resurrection of Jesus Christ to the resurrection of the Christian believers at the Second Advent of the Lord upon the last trumpet that will be sounded by the arch angel. But a believer has to lead a Holy life in obedience to the commandment of Jesus for this great purpose.

The Easter Songs come under two headings. One is 'Easter Songs' and the other is ' Jesus resurrection Songs'. These songs are grouped in the numbers from 162 to 166, 205, 222, 223, .250, 304 & 305 in the 'Christian Songs of Joy' song book..

Apart from being sung in the 'Easter Sunday Services' these song are sung in the Gospel crusades to proclaim the resurrection truth of Lord Jesus Christ. They can be sung on Sunday Services also because the very reason for the Church of Jesus Christ gathering on Sunday the first day of the week is to commemorate the resurrection of Jesus Christ which took place on the first day of the week.

A soul thrilling inspiring songs of Sister Sarah Navaroji on this topic is presented here.

Song No. 162 in the ' Christian Songs of Joy ' song book.

Song No. 162 – Christian Songs of Joy

Chorus

Uyirthezhundaarae Alleluah

Jeyithezhundarae
Uyirudan ezhunda Meetper Yeasen
Sontha maanarae

Stanzas

1.   Kallarai
thiranthidavae   Mathew 28: 2-
4

Kadum sevakar bayanthidavae
Vallavar Yesu Uyirthezhuntharae
Vallappithavin   seyalithuve   -
Uyirthezhuntharae
6. Parisutha maaguthalai

Bayathodendrum
kathukkolvom   I Thess 3:13
Ekkalam   thonikkayil
maruroopamaaga   I Cor 15: 52

Ezhumbuvomae
magimayilae   - Uyirthezhuntharae

Hi- Lights of the song

Victoriously my Jesus the Saviour has risen from the death and has become my own,

states the song's beginning lines.

Stanza 1:- Ref: Mathew 28: 2 to 4 The guards were so afraid that with such a shake the tomb has opened and Jesus arose. This is the act of the mighty Father.

Stanza 6:- Ref: I Cor 15: 52 at the last trumpet we shall be changed and raised in glory,

(I Thessalonians 3:13) so let us keep up our holiness.

6) JESUS' SECOND COMING SONGS

The final hope of a Christian believer is the Second coming of Lord Jesus Christ to consummate all his/her earthly sufferings for righteousness and bestow an eternal abode with everlasting peace and joy. It is according to the Holy Bible verse written in Isaiah 35: 10,

" The ransomed of the Lord shall return, and come to Zion with songs and everlasting joy upon their heads: they shall obtain joy and gladness, and sorrow and sighing shall flee away."

 In the first advent of Jesus Christ he came as a Saviour in the form of an ordinary suffering Son of Man, yet as a Son of God to give Salvation to mankind from sin, sickness and curse. In the second advent, Jesus Christ will come, rather return, as a Judge in the form of a King of Kings who will make war and win and execute judgment over Satan and the Nations that followed him.

Sister Sarah Navaroji has produced a number of soul shaking songs on this particular topic.She was careful to maintain her methodology of impregnating the Bible verses extensively in the songs to bring out the actual truth as said in the scripture about the second coming of Lord Jesus Christ. In doing so, she has achieved in bringing the real scene of Jesus' return on the clouds that one who sings and hears these songs would feel that he or she is present in that very occasion of Jesus coming down on the earth.

The Second Coming songs are found in Numbers 183 to 198 , 208 , 224 , 264 , 345 , 346, 377 & 379 in the ' Christian Songs of Joy' Song book.

The Second Coming songs are composed on all the stages incorporated in the event.

The secret coming, the 7 years of anti Christ rule, the Thousand years rule of Jesus with his saints on this earth, the final battles, formation of New earth, New heaven and

New Jerusalem
and all such intricate matters are vividly described
according to the Holy Bible.
The splendor of heaven in its final form as said in the
book of revelation is elegantly described in the song
composed by Sister Sarah Navaroji that those who sing
and hear these songs ascend to the fourth dimension.
A songs is chosen on this topic to be an example for all
other songs.
The Song admonishes and edifies the listener to live a life
worthy to be raptured or taken up in the second coming
of Lord Jesus Christ.
Song No.191 in the 'Christian Songs of Joy' song book
follows:-
Song No.191 –Christian Songs of Joy

Chorus

Karthar Yesu varuvaar – Niththam
Kaathu thavikkum theva puthirar
Kalippai   Vaanathil   sernthidavae
Romans 8: 23

Stanzas

1.   Megathil   thondrum
vinnoliyil   Mathew 24:27
Magimai Kiristhu velippaduvaar
Thootha   thoni
aaravaarathudan   I Thess 4: 16
Deva ekkalam muzhangidumae
- Karthar

3. Tham manavaatti aayathamae
Thudiyae seluthi magizhnthidavae

Neethi vilangum nal ven vasthiram   Rev 19: 7

Jothiyilanga tharithiduvaal

- Karthar

Hi- Lights of the Song

Quoting Romans 8:23 that the children of God groan inwardly and wait for their adoption as sons,

the song writer says that Lord Jesus will comedown so that they will be gathered in heaven rejoicing.

Stanza 1 – Quotes the saying of Jesus in Mathew 24: 27 that the appearance of Christ will be as the lightning comes from east to west and seen by all. Further, it is quoted from I Thessalonians 4: 16 that with the voice of the archangel and the sound of the trumpet will the Lord come down from heaven.

Stanza 3 – Quoting Revelation 19: 7 says that the Bride has made herself ready wearing the fine white linen, bright and clean which is the righteous acts of saints.

Song No.194 in the ' Christian Songs of Joy' song book is about the 1000 years rule of

8) OUT POURING OF THE HOLY SPIRIT SONGS

Out Pouring of the Holy Spirit is the promise of the heavenly Father for the New Testament Church of Jesus Christ. The Promise is seen in the book of Prophet Joel written in Palestine during the years

795 B.C to 755 B.C

in Joel 2: 28 & 29.   'I will pour out my Spirit on all people'.

This promise Jesus has repeated to his disciples after his resurrection.

in Acts 1: 4 & 5 ' Do not leave Jerusalem, but wait for the gift my Father promised, which you have heard me speak about. For John baptized with water, but in few days you will be baptized the Holy Spirit'.

Sister Sarah Navaroji has composed some special songs which are actually prayers asking the Lord to fill the Church or the praying believer by the Holy spirit quoting the scriptural references of God's promise and the incidences when God poured out his anointing on his people at different times in different contexts.

These special songs are found in Nos. 42, 49, 51,129 , 233 & 373   in the

' Christian Songs of Joy' song book. Actually these songs are part of the Prayer songs.

One of the songs on this topic is considered in detail here in the following page.

Song No. 49 in the 'Christian Songs of Joy' song book.

Song No.49 – Christian songs of Joy

    Chorus

Akkini abishagum thanthu

Aavi pozhindidum   Luke 3:16

    Sub Chorus

Pinmaariyudan parisuthaavi

Balamagha irangidumae

    Stanzas

     1. Patrinathae vaan Akkini

           Bakthan eliyah kooppida   II

Kings Ch.1

           Venduthal kettu vaanam thiranthu

            Vallamai   ootridumae   -

indru   - Akkini

        6. Yiruedu madangu akkini

        Intha kadaisi naatkalil

           Maamisa   maana   yavarin

melum   Joel 2: 28
                         Maariyudan   pozhium   –   pin
           - Akkini

Hi- Lights of the song

Pour out your Spirit of fire anointing , starts the song referring to Luke 3:16

Stanza 1 – II Kings Ch.1 – As the heavenly fire kindled when Prophet Elijah called out, so do pour out your power, opening the heaven to-day, listening to our prayers.

Stanza 6 – Joel 2: 28 – Prayer is to pour out the Spirit of later rain as promised that the Lord will pour out His spirit on all flesh in the last days.

9) PSALMS BASED SONGS(rq;fPjk; ghly;fs;)

Sister Sarah Navaroji has composed, tuned and sung several songs based on the individual Psalms written and sung by different authors mostly by David in the Bible. List of those wonderful songs are presented here with the number of that particular song in the song book .

S.No	Song Psalms No.	Song Title (Transliterated Tamil) Title	Psalm Chapter &Author
1.	113	Thalaimurayai Yendrendrumai Throughout all Generations	90 (Moses)
2.	114	Vasalgale Ungal thalaigalai Lift up your heads O'gates	24 (David)
3.	115	Kalaium Malaium Lord is my Light	27 (David) The
4.	116	Kartharin Saththam Voice of the Lord	29 (David) The

5.   117   Ekkalathum   Kartharai   34
(David)   I   will   Exalt   the   Lord   all   times

6.   118   Mangala Keethangal   45 (
-----   )   Songs   of   Goodness

7.   119   Devan Nam Adaikkalam   46 (-----
)   God is our refuge
8.   120   Unnadamanavarin   Uyarmaraivil
91(David)   He who dwells in the
9.   121   Itho yeredukkirain   121 (---
--)   I will lift up my eyes
10.   225   Asirvathitharulum   128 (-----)
    Blessed   are
all

11.   227   Devane en Devanae   63
(David)   O'God you are my God
12.   228   Karthar Periyavar   48 (----
--)   Great is the Lord
13.   256   Karthar Veettai kattaragil   127
(Solomon)   Unless   the   Lord
builds

14.   257   En Aathumavae nee Kartharai   103
(David)   Praise   the   Lord   O'   my   soul

15.   260   Yeraduppane en kangal   121
(-----   )   I   will   lift   up   my
eyes

16.   387 Jadhigalae Ellorum Kartharai   117 (---
---)   Praise the Lord all you

nations

Song No.114 in the 'Christian Song of Joy' is considered here.
The whole of Psalm Chapter No.24 is composed into a melodious Song. Some Stanzas are shown here.

Song No.114. Christian Songs of Joy   Psalm Ch.24

Ve

rses

      Chorus
Vaasalgalae ungal thalaigalai –nal
Vanjaiudane Uyarthidungal   7a, 9a
      Sub Chorus
Anathi kathaugalae uyara
Anathi Devan utpravesippar   7b, 9b
      Stanzas
1. Senaigalin Karthar ivarthane
   Senathipathiyai vanthaluvaar
   Uththathil vallavar maara magibanae
      Youdhavin   Raja   utpravesippar   -
Vaasalgalae   8, 10

3. Kartharudaiya parvathathilae
   Bakthan parisuthan yar eruvaan
   Poorana vadivu seeyonilae vaazhum

Poorana   Devan   utpravesippar   -
Vaasalgalae   3
4. Ullamathilae Masillathavan
    Unmai parisutha kaigaludan
    Mayai kabadulla aanai agatriyae
        Maa   Devanodae   utpravesippan   -
Vaasalgalae   4
Summary
Only those with a pure heart, clean hands and a blameless soul can enter into the Kingdom of God.Those who seek the face of God are challenged to wide open their hearts (gates).
10) OTHERS
There are many other Topics under which Sister Sarah Navaroji has composed and sung songs.For each and every occasion of Christianity and Christian life we can find appropriate songs in the 'Christian Songs of Joy' song book authored by Sister.
Some of the other topics are such as

NEW YEAR SONGS,
EVANGELISM SONGS ,
MATRIMONIAL SONGS
 FUNERAL SERVICE SONGS.

One song for each of these topics is considered in the following pages.
NEW YEAR SONG
Song No. 36 – Christian Songs of Joy
        Chorus

Karthanai Vaazhthugirein – Avar
Kirubaigal ennidam thanga
Nanmai niraintha Aandithuvae
Nandriyum ponga paadiduvein

Stanza
2. Aandugal thorum vaakkuthatham
Aandavar anbai eanthiduvaar
Kartharai nambiyae thidamanathai
Kadanthiduvein
evvandinaium   - Karthanai

I Praise God for all the goodness and Promises He gives me afresh every year.

EVANGELISM SONG

Song No 347 – Christian Songs of Joy

Chorus

Naam Kartharukku oozhiyam seithiduvom
Nam jeevanulla natkalellam

Sub Chorus

Intha ulaga mai ratchagar Yesuvallal
Ratchippar   veru yarumillai   Acts 4: 12
Paava   saaba   rogangal   seluvaiyil sumanthaar
Baliyaga   namakkaga marithuyirthaar

Summary

Jesus Christ is the only true saviour of the world and there is no one else (Acts 4: 12) because he has borne our Sin, sickness and curse on the cross ,died and rose again.

Let us serve the Lord so that people may hear the good news of salvation , repent, accept the Lord and become believers.

MATRIMONIAL SONGS

Song No. 106 – Christian Songs Of Joy

Stanzas

1. Aathma nesar Yesuve aadhi anthamum neerae
   Aaviyin aasirvatham vanthirungavae
   Mana makkal meethile maariyai pozhiumae
   Mangalam mangalam indrum endrumae

Chorus

Engal Manaalanaam Yesuvirkae

Mangalam endru naam aarparithumae

Inbamaga keetha vaathiyangalodae

Ingithamai paadiyae maghizhuvom

;

2. Intha nal vivaagathin inba thambathigal male
   Unthanin anbu karam neetidum Deva
   Unthan sitham seithumae inba nadu sellavae
   Unnatha eavugal thantharulumae   - Engal

Song Translated in English

1. O! Jesus the beloved of our soul, shower your blessings upon this wedding couple.With melodious musical instruments we shall sing and bless our eternal bride groom Jesus for ever.

2. Stretch out your loving hands O'God upon this sweet couple and reward them with your gifts.

FUNERAL SERVICE SONG - Eternal Hope

Song No.110 – Christian Songs of Joy

Chorus

Deva saayal aaga maari
Devanodiruppain   - Naanum
    Stanza

                    2.   Boomiyin   koodaram
endrum   2   Corinth
5:1

                Belaveename azhinthidumae
                Kaivelaiyallatha pon veedu

                                Kandadainthu
vaazhnthiduven   - Deva
Song Translated in English
Transformed into the image of God ,I will be with God.
2. The earthly tent is always weak and will perish. I will find the Golden house not
    made of hands and shall dwell there.(Stanza 2) II Corinthians 5: 1

5.5 WITNESS OF CHURCH LEADERS

Sister Sarah Navaroji had been specially sealed by the Spirit of God to create unique Christian Songs which as Paul says in I Corinthians 2:5 , are not with enticing words of human wisdom but in demonstration of the Spirit and Power of God. There is no wonder that multitudes have repented and turned to Christ taking up Holy Life, countless have received solace in their troubles ,delivered from sickness,curses and clung to Jesus after being touched by these miraculous songs. Further more, there are numerous people who have dedicated themselves to Serve the Lord as Pastors, Preachers and evangelists and so o

Here are some Church Leaders giving their testimony how they were inspired by the Songs of this great divine poetess.

a) Bishop. D.POTHIRAJULU
 Sister Sarah Navaroji's songs are centered in the truth according to the Bible Verse Acts 4: 12
"There is none other Name ……… whereby we must be saved".
The song in transliterated Tamil
'Umpaadam panindaen - yennalum thudhiyae
  Ummaiyandri yaraippaduvaen - yessaiah
            (meaning)
'I bowdown thy feet – praise you all day long
'Jesus my Master – whom else   do I sing'
is the best example to illustrate it.
My mother got this song sung for her during her last days and passed away to be with the Lord! The beauty of Sister's
songs are that the fire of Holy Spirit is in them. I am

Rt. Rev. Dr.D. Pothirajulu

personally blessed by the song ministry of Sister Sarah Navaroji

and it had elevated my spiritual life to higher and higher standards!. May God continue to use her for many more years !

Bishop. Pothirajulu

b) Bishop JAYASEELAN JACOB

Sister Dr. Sarah Navaroji's song ministry needs a special mention among her other ministries.
While I was a young Pastor I use to fondly listen to her

songs in
L.P. records and then in cassettes.
In the year 1978, I was ordained as Bishop of Tamil Evangelical Lutheren Church. The very next year (1979), I became very sick and had to undergo Cardiac Surgery at Govt. General Hospital , Chennai.

Rt. Rev. Dr.Jayaseelan Jacob

The day before the surgery, Sister Sarah Navaroji visited me in the hospital ward and sung the heart melting song.,

'Inba keetham thunba naeram
 Yindire en yesuve   Song No. 54
        (meaning)
 'The song of Joy at the time of sorrow
        You   gave   me   my   Jesus'

and then prayed for me. I felt like the visitation of an angel of God.The surgery was done successfully by the grace of God and Sisters' Prayers. After the surgery the Lord enabled me to serve him for 15 years of active service. Even today after my retirement from Church Service, I am serving the Lord!   May God Bless Sister Sarah Navaroji!.
Amen! Lord Jesus Come ! Rev. 22: 20.

c)   Rev.   J.G.   JACOB   SUNDER   SINGH, B.Sc.,B.D.,M.Th.,(D.Th)
LUTHEREN   CHURCH,   Poraiyur, Thrangampadi,Nagapattinam.

From the year 1960 , Sister Sarah Navaroji has made a great impact in the Christian world by her melodious , heart melting, divine inspired songs.

Songs like,

Ennai maravaa yesunadha

(meaning)
Jesus you'll never forget me

Deva prasannam tharumae

(meaning)
O God give thy presence

Paavikku pugalidam yesu ratshagar

(meaning)
Jesus the Saviour a refuge for sinner
will never vanish from my heart.One particular song that has been

Rev. J.G. Jacob Sunder Singh

a boost to my spiritual life I want to mention here,

'Pudhu yennaiyaal, pudhu belaththal (meaning) 'with new Oil, new strength

Pudhiya kirubai pudhu kaviyaal   new grace and new song

Nirappi nitham nadathugindreer   you are filling me leading everyday

Noothana saalemil searthiduveer   and will bring me to the new Saalem.'
In my Gospel preaching and singing ministry , when I use to sing Sister's songs like.

Sathiya vedam baktharin keetham   * Scripture of truth ,the Song for godly
Anaadhi devan un adaikkalamae   * Eternal God is thy refuge

many people surrender their lives to Jesus with conviction and tears.

'Magnify the Lord with me, and let us exalt His Name together' Psalm 34: 3, Amen!

Rev. J.G.Jacob Sundersingh

Though we desire to bring in more of this kind of valuable testimonies to boost your faith in the Lord ,we are constrained to restrict ourselves due to the limited space and time that this earth revolves around with.

CHAPTER 6 - Literacy

Human Professionalism and
Divine Intervention in the Literacy

6.1 Introduction

Sister Sarah Navaroji is a gifted poetess in the Christian Mission field. The gift is attributed to her

from two sources. One source is from her earthly father Solomon Asirvatham who systematically taught and trained her on Carnatic Music because he was a carnatic music teacher himself. Second source is the heavenly Father who chose her for this special ministry and equipped her through his son Lord Jesus Christ with the gift of composing Holy Spirit inspired Songs.

When we survey the songs of Sister Sarah Navaroji, one is stuck with awe and wonder to observe the rich literary treasure packed in them. Each and every song is a complete creation with all the elements required for a Christian Spiritual Song.

The Salient features of Sister Sarah Navaroji's Songs are:-

Rich Christian tradition

Melodious tune and wordings

Standardized but Simplified Language in Lyrics common for Literates and illiterates.

Appropriate and approved poetic melodies, tunes and beats.

Grammatical perfection of sentences

Abreast with The Holy Bible teachings

Interpretation of the Scripture

Demonstration of the power of the Holy Spirit

The miscellaneous and usual techniques of a poem or lyric employed.

6.2 Human Professionalism

1. The touch of a qualified professional poet and musician is seen in all Sister's songs by virtue of a systematic study under gone by her with the elder sisters through Solomon Asirvatham their Father who was a Carnatic music teacher himself.

2. An added advantage to her proper learning of music is the natural talent she had for writing poems. When she was studying S.S.L.C (High school Final) in Bentick Girls High School, Madras, she composed a song and sung on the topic U.N.O for an inter schools competition that had won the first prize. It was her first experience of presenting to public a song composed by herself.

3. Sister Navaroji also has a natural melodious voice. She was H.M.V (His Master's Voice) company's standard artist and All India Radio use to relay Sister's song regularly in the devotional songs program. Sister preferred to confine her talents to the Glory of Lord Jesus Christ alone.

4. We read in the Bible Ref: 2 Timothy 1:5

'I have been reminded of your sincere faith ,which first lived in your grand mother Lois and in your mother Eunice and……..now lives in you'.

Similarly the natural talent of composing songs were found in Sister Navaroji's grand Father Solomon, uncle Muthuswamy and then found in her Father Solomon Asirvatham. So also the same gift and skill was found with Sister Sarah Navaroji. Refer item nos. 1.3 and 1.4 in Chapter 1.

5. The wordings in the Songs of Sister Sarah Navaroji, even though, is simple to the understanding of a common man, they are in no way an ordinary writings. Grammatical perfection of the sentences is maintained with fine flow of lyrics. This was indeed possible because from the early age she was so fond of Tamil language and had a great admiration to the Tamil scholars and orators like Aringnar Annadurai and developed her own knowledge in Tamil Language.

6. The usual techniques followed in the poetry are well adhered to in the songs of Sister Sarah. The formation of songs with Chorus , Sub-Chorus, Stanzas are found in order. The various types of rhymes such as couplet, triplet rhymes and Rhyme royal are all employed extensively.

7. Sister had 'Passion for God and Compassion for People' which was the driving force behind all her hard work with self interest to write songs .It would not be an exaggeration to say that these creations are a 'Master Piece' to-day.

8. The virtual effect of these songs on countless people who hear and sing them are, they

Promote moral values with simplicity,
Workout soul edification with sanctification, and
Help in Character building with humble humanity.

6.3 Divine Intervention

1. The Holy Bible says that, "Unless the Lord builds the house,

its builders labour in vain"

 Psalm 127:1

With all the human professionalism in tact with the songs of Sister Sarah Navaroji, without the intervention of God, they could not have produced the desired results. The special anointing of the Holy Spirit, revelation on the scriptural verses, the prophetical gift and an enduring spirit are the tools given to Sister Sarah Navaroji from heaven towards performing this great task of Song ministry.

2. Some times the Holy Spirit lays a burden in her heart and the appropriate song proceeds. The Lord supplies the thoughts for wordings. When sister was working in MES (Madras Electricity Board), as usual one day she was distributing tracts in the bus stop. One young girl received the tract, crushed it and thrown it away. Sister was deeply burdened for that soul who has done this act in ignorance. On returning home She wrote the following passionate song that has drawn many dying Souls to Christ.

Song No.62 - Christian Songs of Joy Song Book

Chorus

Ezhai manu uruvai yedutha

Yesu Rajan unnandai nirkiraar

Yetrukkol avarai thalladhae

Stanzas

Kaigalil kaalgalil aanigal kadaava

Kadum mullmudi pon sirascil soodida
Kandhayum nindayum vathanayum sagithaar
Sonthamaana ratham sinthinaar unakkai
Kanivudan unnai azhaikkiraarae   - Ezhai

Meaning of the Song

Jesus the King who took the form of a humble man is standing besides you. Accept him and don't reject him. With nail pierced hands and legs, crown of thorns pressing upon his head, he has suffered rags and ridicule. He shed his own precious blood for you and compassionately invites you.

3. Some times she hears the angels singing. God has given her the ability to capture the tune and words of the singing of the angels. The she complies the song. The day she was anointed by the Holy Spirit, she heard angels singing and also she could hear the noise of angles flapping their wings. She was able to capture the words and tune of the song of angels in her mind and Sister has composed the following delightful song.

Song No 120. CSJ Song Book

Stanzas

Unnadhamaanavarin – Uyar maraivilirukkiravan

Sarvavallavarin nizhalil thanguvaan
Yidhu parama silaakkiyamae
Chorus
Avar settayin keezh adaikkalam pugavae - tham
Siragugalaal mooduvaar

This song is from Psalm 91.

 He who dwells in the secret place of the most high
Will rest in the shadow of the Almighty
This is a great privilege
He will cover you with his feathers – and under
His wings you will find refuge.

4. At one time when Sister had under taken more than 40 days fasting and prayer, she heard Lord Jesus speaking to her. The voice of the Lord prompted her to compose the following glorious song.

Song No.59 - CSJ Song Book

Chorus

Magimaimael magimai adainthiduvaen
Maruroopamaavaen manamadhilae
Magizhnthidavae dharisikkavae paran mugamae

Stanzas

4. Paadam ondrae podum endraen
  Paesum Aandavar thoniyum kaettaen
  Inba vaakkugale enthan bojanamae
  Ennai belappaduthum – Tham Aaviyinaal - Magimai
In this song Sister quotes II Corinthians 3: 18 .

Meaning of the Song;-
  ' I will transform in my mind and change
    from glory to glory to behold
   the face of the Lord.
   I said the feet of the Lord is sufficient for me
   And I heard the voice of my Lord speaking
  My food is his loving words
  Strengthen me by your Spirit !

5. Sister Navaroji does not search for words to compose songs. She extensively quotes the Scripture verses which constitute a major part of the song. Then she interprets the verses in a simple form as she gets the revelation of the scriptural truths from the Lord. The word of God supplies the words and she composes the songs, gives appropriate tunes and sings for the glory of God and redemption of his people.

It is the Divine intervention that makes Sister Sarah Navaroji's songs seasoned with compassion for souls and packed with the power of the Holy Spirit. No wonder the songs have made a lasting impact on the Christian missionary field world wide. The songs are still vibrating and inviting mankind to the only Saviour of the world Lord Jesus Christ.

The work is a combination of Human Professionalism and Divine intervention in unison and therefore the tone and tenor of her songs stand out different to any other song writer's work that we have come across in the contemporary Christian world.

Sister Sarah Navaroji's Poetic creations are Christian Spiritual Songs par excellence.

CHAPTER 7 - A Special Testimony

A Special Testimony by The Close Associate in the Ministry
Sister LALITHA EVANGELINE
Elder Sister of Sister Sarah Navaroji

Sister Lalitha Evangeline8

Zion Gospel Prayer Fellowship Church , Chennai- 10

I am Sister Sarah Navaroji's second elder sister. We are four daughters to our parents. Our eldest Sister Chandra Leela got married at the age of 18.

At the age of 16, I got Government job in the Survey Department as a Typist. My mother Soundaram Asirvatham who was working as a teacher and I have educated my two younger Sisters up to school final (S.S.L.C.) with much hardships in the family because our father expired at our younger age.

My younger Sister Vasantha became a Pharmacist and theyoungest Sister Sarah Navaroji passed her TNPSC exam and got a job in Madras Electricity Service as a Clerk. In a short time both of them resigned their jobs., obeying the call of God and entered full time Ministry joining Ceylon Pentecostal Mission Church . In the early days of Church ministry both of them had to undergo hardships and work a lot because at home they haven't had any household works to do except their studies, since we had domestic servants to do the work.

In the year 1962 my youngest Sister Sarah Navaroji came back to Chennai from Ceylon Pentecostal Mission Church, Ceylon. She along with my mother stayed in my house at Kilpauk and started her ministries like composing songs, proclaiming Gospel etc. During this time she started getting calls from different places to come and preach the Gospel.

Her first call came from Saidapet . Sister Sarah Navaroji's name was printed in wall poster and hand bills for the Gospel meeting for the first time. Just before going to address these meetings she critically fell ill. While I was attending her from the sick bed, she asked me 'Will you also serve the Lord?'. I said 'yes' . Since then I was trying to keep up the word I gave to my Sister. Then, I asked, God to give me a sign by a 'miracle' to confirm that I should join Sister Navaroji to do the ministry.

Once while Sister Navaroji was preparing to go to preach a crusade in Tirunelveli , having inspired by the Spirit,she told me 'Take care of your son. He is about to get into a great danger.' The next day my son did not go to School due to incessant rain. While I was in my office I got a phone call informing me that my son suffered an Electric Shock. I took permission from my office to come home and on my way to home in taxi, I prayed 'Lord, if I see my son safe, I and my son together will serve you.'

As I was approaching my house, to my surprise, I saw my son coming out running playing a kite. What has happened was.... When my son was playing, he came in contact with a live Electric Wire and got Shock. He fell unconscious and a nurse nearby examined him and said 'no pulse'. My mother and sister prayed for the child and took him to K.M.C. hospital nearby. Even as a Doctor was examining him, he suddenly opened his eyes and got down from the bed and started running.

God did a miracle for me that day. Another day when he was walking in the street two boys were fighting throwing stones at each other. One stone struck my son's head rear side and was profusely bleeding. We brought him to Sister Navaroji for prayer. She laid her hand on the wound and prayed. The oozing blood suddenly stopped.

This is the second miracle the Lord did for me to confirm that I should help my younger Sister Sarah Navaroji in her ministry.

Even as Sister Navaroji watched the blood flowing from the wound of the child, she saw in that the bleeding wounds of the Master Lord Jesus Christ and a glorious song gushed out of her.

That wonderful song goes like this:-

'Siluvai sumanda uruvam   (meaning) 'Lo the body bearing   the   cross....

...Sinthina ratham purandodiyea'
Littering blood flowing across....'

and this song has become one of her popular songs not many days later.

In the early days, my mother and I were belong to the Brethren Assembly Church. We do not believe in the anointing of the Holy Spirit and speaking in tongues those days. When my mother believed that the Lord is giving the Holy Spirit to them that ask she received the Holy Spirit. Then, I prayed that the Lord should fill me also with the Holy Spirit but not in a crowd with emotion. So, I took three daysfasting and prayed in my room. I was filled with the Holy Spirit with the sign of speaking in tongues.

Immediately after that, I gave up all my outward adoration of gold and silver jewelry. The love of worldly things have vanished from me. Also I made a dedication to wear only white dress. Since then, I started accompanying my youngest Sister Sarah Navaroji wherever she was going to preach the Gospel. I used to take my two children also along with me.

With us a group of Sisters from our Church would come to sing in the Gospel meetings. They all sing the songs composed by Sister Navaroji referring our song book. But my 10 year old daughter used to sing those songs without seeing the book. To watch this wonder many people will gather well in advance for the meetings. Many people use to surrender their lives to Jesus and get saved in those Gospel campaigns.

Sister Sarah Navaroji encouraged us to pray for the salvation of Nations by placing our fingers on each nation and country on the world map. The good Lord enabled me to go personally to all those countries along with Sister Navaroji to proclaim the Gospel and share our testimonies.

My husband died due to sudden heart failure in the year 1988. Till then, we were serving the Lord together taking care of all Church ministry and Gospel work needs. But later,I took voluntary retirement and started staying with Sister Navaroji and carry on the ministry along with her. My daughter and Son were living in separate houses after their marriage.

My son- in -law Rev. Dr. R. Samuel, after having worked as an Engineer in India and abroad for a long time , now being guided by the Lord, left all his secular assignment to serve the Lord assisting Sister Sarah Navaroji in the Church Ministry. His wife, my daughter plays key board music in the Church Service and arranges for various ministerial activities. My son whom I dedicated for the ministry is taking care of maintaining and operating vehicles (car, van) for Sister Sarah Navaroji and all other needs for the Church.

May all Glory and Honor be unto the Lord!

Sister Lalitha Evangeline